D0996934

Julian Lloyd Webber: Married to Music

The Authorised Biography

By the same author:

Dolmetsch: The Man and his Work
The Great Violinsts
The Great Cellists
Henry Purcell: Glory of His Age

Julian Lloyd Webber: Married to Music

The Authorised Biography

Margaret Campbell

 Robson Books

First published in Great Britain in 2001 by Robson Books, 10 Blenheim Court, Brewery Road, London N7 9NY

A member of the Chrysalis Group plc

British Library Cataloguing in Publication Data
A catalogue record for this title is available from the British Library.

ISBN 1 86105 400 9

Typeset by FiSH Books, London WC1
Printed by Creative Print & Design, Ebbw Vale.

Dedicated to the memory of my husband Dick –
beloved companion for fifty years

Contents

Acknowledgements

I would like to acknowledge the help I have received from my editor, Joanne Brooks, and the following, who have generously given of their time to meet me or write to me: Felix Aprahamian, Celia Ballantyne, Anna Barry, Justine Bax, Pam Chowhan, Charles Collins, Jon Cooke, Mary Garner, Richard Hickox, Michelle Jenkins, Andrew Keener, Jill Lawrence, John Lenehan, John Lill, Zohra Lloyd Webber, Lord Andrew Lloyd Webber, John McCabe, Sir Neville Marriner, Rhuna Martin, David Mellor QC, James Murphy, Jerrold Northrop Moore, Andrew Pledge, Tim Rice and Callum Ross.

Julian allowed me unlimited access to his late mother's unpublished memoirs, which she wrote shortly after the death of her husband. They contained touching accounts of her own early years and some hilarious ones of Julian's childhood. I am also grateful to Julian for diligently researching reviews, correspondence and general information that proved to be invaluable.

Foreword

The early years of Julian Lloyd Webber's life were undisciplined and slightly chaotic but certainly music was always a large part of his background. He had a great talent and won scholarships which gained him the opportunity to benefit from fine teaching.

Although Julian started playing the cello when still very young, it was not until he was twelve years old that he was truly inspired by hearing Rostropovich. In that moment he realised that music and the cello were going to be his life. Now a mature artist, he has some excellent qualities. He is very loyal to his friends and colleagues, to his composer father's memory and to other British composers (many of whom he has championed unremittingly). He writes well and talks graphically, often with a delightful sense of humour. He does not hesitate to say what he feels even though he is fully aware that it may be prejudicial to his own interest.

I knew Jacqueline du Pré very well and saw her frequently during the last ten years of her life. I was touched that Julian was so incensed by the falseness of the recent book and film about her, instigated by her sister and brother. Whether or not they just wanted money I do not know, but certainly they only did harm to Jackie's memory. Julian's activity on her behalf was typical of his convincing honesty and of his commitment to just causes. He is truly a man of integrity – a rare quality today.

I have long admired Margaret Campbell's books, with her musical, flowing style of writing, and her admirably accurate research into everything concerning anyone with whom she is involved. In this wonderful biography she has brought Julian to life in a sympathetically warm and convincing way. It is so vivid and well written that it is not only interesting but an absorbing pleasure to read.

Evelyn Barbirolli
London, 2001

Introduction

I first spoke to Julian Lloyd Webber on the telephone. That delightful man, the late Stephane Grappelli, called me one evening from Malvern where he was appearing in a TV programme with a young cellist whom he thought I should write about. I had interviewed Stephane for inclusion in my book on violinists and written a profile of him in *The Strad* so when he introduced Julian as a worthy subject I could hardly refuse. I fixed a meeting with Julian for the following week and the profile duly appeared. This was in 1981 and from that time onwards I have followed his career with interest for almost twenty years.

I was delighted when I was asked to write his biography and even more delighted when he agreed to allow me unprecedented access to family archives (including his mother's unpublished autobiography) and the freedom to present the true story of his highly unusual family and the attendant problems of growing up within such multi-talented and unorthodox surroundings. When we discussed the project and I told Julian that I wanted *carte blanche* to write a true account, Julian replied: 'But of course...authorised does not mean *sanitised!*' We were off to a good start.

Today, Julian enjoys an international reputation and has played with most of the world's leading orchestras. He has an impressive discography and his recording of the Elgar Concerto with the Royal Philharmonic under Menuhin was voted 'Best British Classical Record of the Year' in the 1987 Brit Awards and was chosen as the 'finest ever recorded version' by the *BBC Music Magazine*. Apart from his playing, perhaps his most important contribution has been his indefatigable research into neglected British music. He has painstakingly ferreted into the archives to retrieve forgotten works by Elgar, Delius and many of his contemporaries, presenting them in concert and subsequently making recordings. He has also premiered many new works for cello and a new concerto is currently being written for him by the American composer Philip Glass.

Julian is also a stylish writer. I have drawn considerably on his *Travels with my Cello* (Pavilion Books, 1984) which contains many hilarious anecdotes highlighting some of the problems of travelling with such a bulky instrument.

What will surprise many people is that Julian is also not afraid to campaign for an important cause. His condemnation of the way in which our children are spoon-fed with pop when they ought to be given the choice of hearing more classical music is something with which many people agree but would be afraid to champion. Another is his absolute rejection of the portrayal of Jacqueline du Pré as manipulative and foul-mouthed in the film *Hilary and Jackie*. I was impressed by the evidence regarding both these issues and, in recounting them, hope that I have treated them objectively.

I must confess that I have enjoyed writing this book – not only because Julian is in himself an interesting personality, but also because I feel I have been given the opportunity to put the record straight. This, for any writer, is a welcome gift.

When I began my researches into the family background I was amazed at how it had been possible for William Lloyd Webber – the father of Julian and Andrew – to have been so neglected as a composer. As many people now realise, Julian has carried out a wonderful service to the world of music by rescuing his father's manuscripts and getting CDs of his music onto the market. The general public can now be aware of this man whose compositions can stand comfortably beside the work of early Delius, early Vaughan Williams, Gerald Finzi, John Ireland, George Butterworth, Roger Quilter, E.J. Moeran and others of the same era. His pessimism and frustration at remaining so unfulfilled led him to deep depression and alcoholism, which obviously had an effect upon his two sons. His wife Jean, a dedicated socialist-Christian was another enigmatic character whose mission in life was to help others. When their family circle was later enlarged to admit the pianist John Lill, the lyricist Tim Rice and several penniless music students, their top floor Kensington flat became seriously overcrowded, not to say cacophonous, with a medley of keyboard, brass and stringed instruments resounding at all times of the day and night.

Nonetheless, the twelve-year-old Julian set his mind on the cello and from that day to this he has never wavered. *Married to Music* is the story of how he made his way to the top and some of the struggles that he had to overcome, not least because his brother was so successful in a different musical field.

Julian has tremendous drive to succeed and is a perfectionist in everything he undertakes. One of his friends told me that once when he was not sure how a certain passage had sounded in a recording, he travelled at his own expense to Holland to visit the Philips studio 'just to make sure'.

I have talked to many of his friends and colleagues and everyone speaks of his loyalty and kindness. Perhaps the most explicit confirmation of this comes from Pam Chowhan, who first met him at the South Bank Centre, where she works today as Programme Planning Manager for the Queen Elizabeth Hall:

'Working with Julian can be challenging! We have worked

together not only on arrangements of pre-existing works but also original material. Julian is extremely fastidious, and his attention to detail is quite monumental – and at times infuriating! He will happily spend half-an-hour on a single chord, exploring all possible permutations, only to decide that the first shot was the best after all. However, his desire for perfection is always tempered with good humour that ensures that the work remains fun.

'Julian is a very private person and his circle of truly close friends is very small. He is very loyal to the few people he really cares about. He's not particularly materialistic or interested in wealth or status, and will make a friend because he "clicks" with someone, not because of who they are. He's very intense, sensitive and introspective, as you might expect an artist to be. On the other hand, there's a very down-to-earth side – he enjoys a pint down at the local along with the next man and football – in the shape of Leyton Orient – has always featured high on his list of priorities.'

Margaret Campbell
Berkhamsted, 2001

Chapter 1

Roots

The Lloyd Webber story begins with two generations of self-employed plumbers who spent every second of their spare time in a musical activity of some kind. Julian and Andrew Lloyd Webber's grandfather, William Charles Henry Webber, lived near the Angel in London but plied his trade in the considerably more affluent Royal Borough of Kensington and Chelsea. His father had played the violin and William could sing almost before he could talk. He had been a chorister from the age of seven and when his voice broke he developed into a fine tenor. Although he stuck to his trade in order to live, in a purely amateur capacity he sang with the Bach Choir, the BBC Chorus, the Black and White Minstrels and the Oriana Madrigal Society. As if this were not enough he was also a member of the choir at All Saints Margaret Street for most of his life.

No doubt a long association with church music inspired William's other musical interest which bordered on an obsession. He was an organ buff who, in his spare time, would travel around London looking at the many splendid instruments in churches and cathedrals and taking notes about their makers and their construction. Above all he loved to listen to their glorious sounds and fast became an authority on 'the king of instruments'.

His son, William Southcombe Lloyd Webber, was born in 1914 and delighted his father by showing an interest in music from babyhood. The story goes that when he was only two years old he was taken to Chester Cathedral to hear the service and from the moment he heard the organ he pestered his father to build one for him. This was no easy matter, but William senior found an old chest of drawers and removed part of the front to accommodate a seat; he would lift his son on to it so he could use the drawer knobs as stops. Young 'Bill' thereafter spent many hours happily playing this imaginary instrument. Very soon he became a chorister and began lessons on the family harmonium. He was also playing the organ and by the age of ten, as 'Master W.S.L. Webber', was already giving recitals at city churches, sometimes providing the accompaniment to his father's singing.

Bill was obviously a very bright child and proved it by winning an organ scholarship to Mercers School, one of the oldest educational establishments in London, founded to provide good schooling for gifted boys from poor families. He was also offered a scholarship to the Royal Academy of Music when he was only fourteen but did not take it up as he could not leave school at such an early age.

By 1929 Bill was already giving broadcasts for the BBC and he was only seventeen when appointed organist at Christ Church, Newgate Street, moving to St. Cyprian's Clarence Gate in 1933. In 1939 he became organist and choirmaster at All Saints' Margaret Street – where his own father was one of the choristers under his control – a position he held until 1948.

The distinguished writer and Music Critic on the *Sunday Times* for over forty years, Felix Aprahamian, first met both father and son at Park Chapel, Crouch End, in 1931 where they had come to see the Father Willis Organ. It was then looked after by the famous Sydney John Ambler who had a job in the Bank of England but whose hobby was the organ. He had a workroom at the back of Park Chapel and people from all over the world would come to visit him. Aprahamian recalls that one Saturday morning he was practising the organ when the two Webbers arrived with a letter of introduction to Ambler. 'Young William, who was my age, sat down on the bench and simply romped his way through the Widor *Toccata* from memory without a single wrong note. Then he sight-read the Joseph Bonnet *Rhapsodie Catalan* that I put on the desk. I remember him playing it impeccably, including the difficult pedal cadenza, without turning a hair.'

That same year Bill won an open scholarship to the Royal College of Music where he was a pupil of Vaughan Williams for composition and Dr Henry Ley, Precentor to Eton College, for organ. As a student he had a brilliant record. On one occasion he played Reger's extremely difficult *Phantasie and Fugue über B-A-C-H* from memory at a College concert only a week after he had been given the score. At nineteen, he also had the distinction of being the youngest ever organist to receive the FRCO diploma, and five years later became the youngest to receive a doctorate.

From a very young age, Bill had started to compose. Although the music that has survived from this period shows the influence of Rachmaninov, César Franck and other late Romantics, it also bears clearly the stamp of his own individual style.

It was at the College that Bill's third Christian name crept in as part of his surname. It seems that at the time there was another organist called W.G. Webber and, in order to distinguish himself, he made the alteration and became William Lloyd Webber.

Since he always had a talent for the keyboard, Bill tended to take it for granted. He had 'perfect pitch' and could read anything from sight so could easily have made a career as an organist and would almost certainly have ended up in one of the great cathedrals. But Bill never wanted to be a cathedral organist. He had many offers, but always refused saying that he did not want to become a part of the establishment. The rebel within him preferred his own independent if somewhat limited life. Much of this attitude was engendered by his upbringing. Having spent his most impressionable years within the Anglo-Catholic church, he became very influenced by its dictates and found them hard to shed. Much later on in his life, his wife asked him what he did for his 21st birthday. His reply left her speechless: 'I went to tea with the vicar.'

As to his gifts as an organist, Felix Aprahamian has no doubts: 'He was a virtuoso. I remember when I was Secretary of the Organ Music Society I engaged Bill to perform the very difficult Fourth Symphony by Louis Vierne at two of London's leading churches, the Temple Church and Holy Trinity Sloane Street, and later on the restored Father Willis organ at the Alexandra Palace. Why? Because he was the only person who could play it and *wanted* to play it!' Despite this outstanding talent, what William Lloyd Webber really wanted to be was a composer and as such he was greatly gifted, as his writings from this early period – such as the 1936 *Fantasie Trio* – clearly show. Felix Aprahamian recalls: 'There is no doubt that as a composer he was a master; there was colour in his organ-playing which was reflected in his writing for the keyboard and colour in his vocal textures which was apparent in his choral works. His misfortune was that he lived at a time when there were so many good English composers. We are dealing with the generation that was before the arrival of Benjamin Britten. We must not forget that composers who were writing in the early part of the twentieth century and right through the twenties and thirties were masters of tonal music. There was a plethora of talent – not only talent but genius, and each one presented an individual musical physiognomy. But there were too many for them all to be remembered. It was the same in France. We've all heard of Debussy and Ravel, but contemporary with these were at least twenty marvellous French composers, again too many of them to find room at the top.'

When the Second World War broke out in 1939 Bill was twenty-five and, in addition to his job at All Saints Margaret Street, he made some extra money by playing the organ in cinemas for the silent films, improvising on the spot to suit the action. He also served for five years in the Royal Army Pay Corps.

It was at All Saints in 1939 that he first met Jean Johnstone, who was then studying at the Royal College of Music. She and a number of other students had been appointed as stand-ins for the absent boy trebles who had been evacuated. She promptly developed a 'crush' on the handsome young choirmaster and three years later they were married at the church where they had first met.

Jean Hermione Johnstone's background could not have been more different from that of her future husband's. She was the daughter of Charles Campbell Johnstone, a major in the Argyll and Sutherland Highlanders and Laura Mary Johnstone, always known as Molly. It had been an arranged marriage which Molly resented from the start and the story goes that on her wedding night she threw her ring down the lavatory. Not surprisingly it was a disastrous union – according to Molly her husband was 'wild, irresponsible and impossible'. Nonetheless she bore him three children – a son, Alastair, and two daughters, Viola and Jean, but after ten years she could stand it no longer and, creating major waves for her time, divorced him and moved south to live in Harrow-on-the Hill, where her son attended the famous public school.

Molly was an idealistic, deeply religious woman who regularly attended the City Temple Church where the distinguished preacher Leslie Weatherhead was minister. She also championed that other great left-wing Methodist, Donald Soper.

Her three children were entirely different in character.

Viola, the eldest, always known as 'Vi' was outgoing and extrovert and eventually became an actress. Although she is reputed to have appeared with John Gielgud and other famous actors, she never achieved anything but small parts, although she did produce a rather risqué recipe book called *The Hostess Cooks*. Alastair was sensitive and artistic with considerable talents as a poet and naturalist, who showed early promise of a brilliant future. Jean – five years younger than her brother – was intensely shy and introvert. In 1935 the family experienced a tragedy which had a profound and traumatic effect from which neither Molly nor Jean ever fully recovered. Alastair was just eighteen and about to take up his place at Cambridge, when he went on a bird-watching expedition with a friend in Dorset. One afternoon, they decided to take a boat out to sea but they had underestimated the very strong currents. Alastair was swept overboard. His companion managed to return to shore and raise the alarm, but Alastair's body was never found.

As soon as Molly heard the news she rushed to Dorset with Vi, leaving the thirteen-year-old Jean behind with her aunt Felicia and her grandmother. Jean and Alastair had been soulmates and she was inconsolable. Even as a grown woman she could remember the agony of lying on her bed sobbing hysterically for days on end, unable to believe she would never see him again. Possibly the saddest outcome was that she began to feel unwanted herself. Her sister Vi was grown up and could be a companion to her mother, but she could do little to help. Alastair had been the only son, and a brilliant one at that; gradually she began to think her mother had wished it had been her instead of Alastair who had died.

Many years later, Jean wrote about her increasing preoccupation with the idea of being unwanted. This grew in her imagination so much that it became an obsession and led to a deep feeling of insecurity. 'Looking back, it must have been an appalling time for my mother, as not only did she have to bear the grief of Alastair's loss, but also my reaction to it. Vi was also under great strain and, as a result, she became irritable and impatient with me.'

Molly could no longer bear to live in Harrow with all its associations so, within a few weeks, their beautiful home – a 12-roomed freehold detached house with a large garden – was sold for £1700, and they moved to London. Jean was devastated. Not only had she lost her brother but also had to leave a school where she had been very happy and start life anew within the confines of a London flat.

All this had a profound psychological effect. As a teenager she was still acutely shy and self-effacing and getting to know her proved extremely difficult. In later years people remained unaware of the fact that, as a student at the College, she had shown great promise. She studied composition with Vaughan Williams and violin with William Reed, a close friend and biographer of Elgar who was also leader of the London Symphony Orchestra for many years. After her marriage she devoted her time to teaching piano to very young children, with whom she could communicate much better than with adults. Her awkward manner did not endear her to people, though once they got to know her they found her to be a trusted and loyal friend who could always be called upon for help. She was totally without vanity and never interested in fashion; in fact, most of her clothes were bought from charity shops or jumble sales. She had also inherited her mother's socialist-Christianity and her main mission in life was to help anyone in need; her concern for the under-privileged of the world was obsessive and occasionally led to the neglect of her own offspring.

Once her children had finished their schooling, Molly took on a job as a doctor's receptionist and very soon fell in love with her employer. It is not known how far the romance progressed, but as soon as the doctor set eyes on Molly's daughter, the effervescent Vi, he was immediately attracted and soon they were married. Vi promptly retired from the stage and moved to take up residence in Weymouth Street, in that fashionable part of London that is devoted to the medical profession. Poor Molly had been cheated for the second time.

As for Bill, the general effect of the Blitz, combined with his musical and army activities meant that he had less and less time for composition, but as soon as the hostilities ceased he started writing again. This was to be his most prolific period, but sadly it did not meet with the success he had hoped.

As Felix Aprahamian explained, it was a fate shared by many other aspiring composers. In any form of creative work, persistence is the key factor, and those who have the drive either achieve some success or find some other forms of expression. Bill was a born pessimist and soon began to regard himself as a failure. Jean did everything she could, and more, to encourage him but he would not be pushed. Later he became very bitter and felt that, despite the fact he had done his best for his country during the war, he was not recognised for what he was worth. He would cite the case of Benjamin Britten who spent the early war years safely in the US and returned to have his first opera *Peter Grimes* successfully produced at Covent Garden. So great was Bill's disappointment that later he discouraged his two sons from following a career in music. He would tell them that it was a 'terrible profession' and that life would always be difficult. 'Enter music as a last resort and only if there is absolutely nothing else you can do,' he said.[1]

Fortunately it was advice that neither of them heeded.

Chapter 2

Life at the Top

The London flat to which Molly had brought her family in 1935 was Number 10, Harrington Court, adjacent to South Kensington Underground Station. It was one of those large, somewhat dilapidated Victorian red brick buildings which were fortunately a great deal more sturdily built than their counterparts today. This was just as well when the newly-weds moved in. Molly, who was by this time very deaf, needed to have the television turned up to full volume; Bill had had an electric organ installed and Jean had now given up the violin in favour of the piano. Their long-suffering neighbour who occupied the flat on the floor below was the actor Carleton Hobbs, famous for his interpretation of Sherlock Holmes in a long-running BBC radio series.

In order to supplement her husband's modest income, Jean took on a job at Wetherby School in Rosary Gardens only a few minutes walk from their flat, where she taught piano and singing. The rest of the day would be devoted to her private pupils – children in the day and adults in the evening, often up to ten o'clock. It was Molly who cleaned and prepared meals and, later, when the children arrived, it was Molly who looked after them.

Bill continued to play the organ at All Saints and in 1946 became a professor at the Royal College of Music. The little time he had left was spent locked in his room composing. A work dating from this time was his children's musical, *Pinocchio*, which was staged successfully by students at the College. His output during this period was prolific, but seldom met with success from the publishers. One rejection was too much for him and the score would be stuffed in a drawer and forgotten. Jean, who had always believed in his talent, did her best to encourage him, but Bill was one of the world's natural-born pessimists. He *did* have a great sense of humour and on occasions could be hilarious. But he was also prone to dramatic changes of mood and, when he was in a fit of depression, nothing could drag him back to normality.

This situation was not helped by Jean's concern for anyone in need of help. She always seemed to have some worthy cause or another on hand and through her work with displaced persons, she came into contact with some refugees from Gibraltar. These included a rather handsome young man named Luis who – according to Jean – had a wonderful tenor voice. After most of the Gibraltarians had been repatriated, Luis (no-one seems to remember his surname) remained as he had been given a British Council scholarship to study with Alfred Piccaver. Julian maintains that his mother had a fixation on him and that his father was certainly not happy about it. He was a frequent visitor to Harrington Court as Jean would accompany him when he was learning the operatic repertoire. She insisted that he was a great undiscovered singer, but there are no recordings – or any other evidence – that this was so. Finally the excitement waned and Luis disappeared.

However, on one occasion he did manage to ingratiate himself with Bill. He arrived at the flat one day with apologies for being late. 'Sorry,' he said, 'but I've been playing with Mimi.'

'Who on earth is Mimi?' asked Bill.

'Oh, she's the monkey. Some Polish sailors who live in the

next room to me brought her back from Bombay.' He then recounted Mimi's life history. It seems that she and her companion male monkey were running wild in the streets of Bombay, took a fancy to the sailors and began to follow them everywhere. So they decided to adopt the pair and called them Mimi and Rodolfo (the lovers from Puccini's *La Bohème*). It seems that Rodolfo was rather more adventurous than Mimi and had managed to fall overboard on the voyage back to England leaving poor Mimi heartbroken. Luis told Bill that the sailors had soon to rejoin their ship, so they needed a home for her. Bill's reaction was unexpected, to say the least. 'I must see her now. Can we go?' Operatic repertoire was instantly forgotten and both Jean and Bill set off for Luis' digs.

When Luis opened the door of the Poles' room Mimi was perched on top of the curtain rail. As soon as she saw them she began chattering indignantly to herself, and Bill, who adored animals of any species, was completely charmed. Jean, too, appeared totally smitten. 'It was love at first sight for both of us,' she recalled.

'I'll have her,' said Bill. 'We'll take her home as soon as possible.' The Poles were out at the time but next day Luis appeared with Mimi in tow – complete with harness, lead and a large cage, which the sailors had made out of cord.

Mimi's cage was duly erected in the drawing room along with blankets and an electric fire to keep her warm at nights. From the beginning, Bill was devoted to her. Jean remembered how she would flirt with him outrageously and would hold hands for hours if given the chance. She also had some bad habits. Her favourite toilet was on the top of the grand piano, and she would make herself a constant source of annoyance to the neighbours – finding her way into their flats and stealing everything from gold chains to jam tarts.

Mimi was always very affectionate towards Jean, and it came as a shock when she suddenly turned against her and flew at her at every opportunity. She remained friendly towards Bill and everyone else, which made it even more of a mystery. A few weeks later Jean discovered she was pregnant and came to the conclusion that Mimi had known this before she did and had become jealous. Jean had suffered a miscarriage a few years previously – a traumatic experience which had left its mark. When she was carrying her second child she became increasingly nervous of Mimi, who, with that incredible animal instinct, had become even more vicious. One day she attacked Jean so fiercely that the Lloyd Webbers decided she would finally have to go. For a time Mimi was handed on to their postman but eventually – when she became older and more difficult – she was taken into the Withdean Zoo in Brighton.

When Andrew arrived in 1948 he proved to be hyper-active, vociferous and constantly in need of attention, which Jean somehow managed to blame on Mimi. Later, when Andrew was forty, rich, famous and the subject of *This is Your Life* on television, Jean said: 'He never stopped screaming until – well, just about now.' Bill went further: 'He was forever jumping and bumping around the place, making a dreadful din and disturbing all the neighbours at three o'clock in the morning.' The only successful soporific was the Latin American dance music of Edmundo Ros and his band. Bill would place records on his creaky, wind-up gramophone while Jean tried to rock the 'little terror' to sleep.[2]

Their second son, Julian, was born on 14 April 1951, and his parents viewed his arrival with some apprehension wondering whether they were in for another noisy and sleepless few years. Apparently, Julian did not scream quite as violently as Andrew and even slept occasionally, but it was soon obvious that he had boundless energy which never seemed to flag – so a new set of problems were posed. As soon as Julian began to walk he required constant surveillance. Electric points proved a source of great interest when he discovered that objects could be inserted into the sockets. Wooden boxes had to be built around each one, with sliding fronts and a key so that the plugs could be reached when necessary. As they were not exactly an organised household at the best of times, the key would sometimes be mislaid and tempers would become frayed.

Julian also developed a fascination with dropping things over the balcony. Thrown from the top floor, objects would make a satisfying crash when they reached the ground and Julian would squeal with delight. One day he went a bit too far and hurled a large carving knife over the top: to everyone's relief there was no innocent passer-by below to meet with an untimely death. A further absorbing interest was finding out how thick the walls were and, having discovered a drill, he once spent several happy hours boring a hole into the outside wall from the balcony. He was caught just in time to prevent the hole from becoming deep enough to penetrate the room inside.

Perhaps the most alarming of Julian's escapades was at the age of four when the family were on holiday in the New Forest. They had rented a cottage on the edge of the forest and set off in their ancient Rover, which they parked among the trees outside. One day Jean looked out of the window and saw with horror that the car was moving. She thought at first that they had forgotten to put on the brake and rushed to the front door. She was even more shaken when she saw Julian at the wheel. Seconds later, the car plunged even more swiftly, crashed through some foliage and came to an abrupt halt against a tree. Julian had obviously decided to do a little experiment with driving but, although the front of the Rover was smashed, he had somehow remained intact. Julian was unabashed as usual but his mother was in a state of shock when she realised that, had the tree not put an end to the experiment, the car and its driver would have ended up on the busy Bournemouth Road.

Music at home was part of the scenery and the two boys

took it for granted. However, despite her undoubted success with all her other young pupils, Jean had little with her own sons. From the age of three, Andrew was picking his way on the keyboard by ear but was not interested in any formal lessons, which drove his mother to despair. She complained that he *always* played in a completely unorthodox manner: 'All the pieces he was supposed to play, he wouldn't touch. He wanted to play his own tunes and no others!' She was equally disappointed by her younger son. Julian recalls that he was seated in front of the piano when he was four and hated every minute of it; mainly because he found it extremely difficult to get both his hands working together. Later he was taken to one of the Ernest Read Children's Concerts at the Royal Festival Hall where they played the *Sorcerer's Apprentice*. Julian was riveted by the sound of the cellos in the orchestra and instantly asked if he could have one. He later admitted that another idea had also occurred to him: 'I thought that if I began playing another instrument, I'd be allowed to give up the dreaded piano.'

Julian's first lessons were with Alison Dalrymple who had a direct, forthright manner, but great humanity and understanding of her pupils. She had a well-deserved reputation for teaching the very young and a few of her pupils went on to become famous soloists, the most celebrated being Jacqueline du Pré. She fitted Julian up with a minute cello, not much bigger than a viola, which she lent to him because it was the only one so small in her possession. When it arrived, Julian was deeply disappointed because it in no way represented one of those magnificent objects he had seen that day at the Festival Hall. He was told it was very suitable for a boy of five so, thoroughly disgruntled, sat down to play it. From the onset he liked the sound that it made and soon he was spending as much time as possible with his new toy, making sure there was none left to go anywhere near the piano. In *Travels with my Cello* Julian quotes his mother's recollections of what these lessons were like; although naturally he claims the account to be totally fictitious:

Parents used to be encouraged to stay during the lessons and, as they were mostly musicians themselves, to accompany their offspring on the piano. This I did, but the lessons were usually a nightmare for me because Julian could not keep still at all, while everybody else's children seemed able to. He had an irritating way of doing things wrong on purpose and watching intently to see if he was creating the desired effect. When he found he was he would roar with laughter and jump on and off his small stool while mother nearly died of embarrassment.

Once Alison suggested that it might be "fun" to combine a lesson with another small pupil. My heart *sank*. There was nothing I could do about it. But Julian thought it was hilarious, especially when they played together and were told to count when they had bars of rests. He found that by counting in a slightly different time he could upset the proceedings in a profoundly satisfactory manner. The final straw came when his excitement reached fever pitch and, leaping on to the stool, he started attacking the other child with his bow in an elaborate fencing motion at which point Alison screamed in horror, "Julian, dear, it's your precious bow, not a sword!"

Nevertheless, he redeemed his reputation at one of the periodical concerts held in a hall in Duke Street, when he played a short piece from his very first solo book, dressed in a pale blue silk shirt and navy velvet shorts. This completely captivated the audience, and one man was heard to remark, "Oh, isn't he *divine*". Actually he played quite well too and, for once, seemed to be concentrating.[3]

Another unnerving experience for Jean was when the five-year-old Julian took his first Associated Board cello exam. He and his mother made their way to the stately Royal Academy of Music, Jean carrying his little stool as the usual chairs were much too high. The examiners seemed to be very serious and were not at all amused at the sight of this small child who seemed to be taking it all in his stride. The music stands were much too high, so with his mother accompanying him, Julian played everything from memory and, after the exam, appeared to be quite satisfied with his performance. Jean, who had been ordered to leave the room during the sight-reading test, was concerned, thinking that the examiner would have had to hold the music up or place it on a chair. 'Oh! I couldn't see *that*!' said Julian. 'It was on the stand and it was much too high.' Jean asked nervously how he had managed. 'Oh, I just made it up. It was quite all right.' The marks for that section did not confirm his self-confidence, but for once it was not his fault.

Another occasion could have brought about a very premature end to the budding young cellist's career. Jean had organised a sixth birthday party for Julian and, contemplating the thought of a bunch of wild infants rushing around the flat, she hit on the idea of hiring a slide from nearby Harrods which she hoped would keep them entertained. Julian was mad with excitement and, as soon as the first guest rang the bell, he dashed along the hall, banged his hand on the glass front door pane, whereupon it smashed right through. Blood was spurting everywhere and a doctor was immediately summoned. Julian spent the rest of his 'party' in bed, his face ashen while the doctor inserted stitches into his left hand: the stitch-marks are clearly visible today.

Andrew was meanwhile a great deal closer to his ebullient Aunt Vi than he was to his mother, and when he began to show an interest in the theatre, Vi was the one who encouraged him. When he was only nine years old she supervised the construction of a toy theatre built with bricks and wooden blocks. The walls were wallpapered with 'samples' from Sanderson's showrooms and a red-plush curtain could be drawn as in a real theatre. A revolving stage was made from a gramophone turntable imitating television's *Sunday Night at the London Palladium*. Andrew, who acted as general factotum, was composer, writer and stage manager. He also played his tunes on the piano while six-year-old Julian obediently moved the 'cast' of toy soldiers around the set. The audience – consisting of members of the family and one or two unsuspecting friends – applauded enthusiastically as the final curtain was lowered. Julian remembers that the music for one of these early songs has survived in what was to be Andrew's first outstanding success, *Joseph and the Amazing Technicolour Dreamcoat*.

One of the things conspicuous by its absence in the Lloyd Webber household was discipline. The two boys were allowed to go their own way, make their own decisions and never made to practise. In some ways this encouraged them to develop their own personalities but it could also be dangerous. If they wanted to wander off and explore they were never prevented from doing so. When Julian was only nine years old this proved disastrous. One of his favourite passions was the London underground. He knew every line and every station by heart and it was his ambition to travel to every single one on the map. One afternoon he boarded a Piccadilly line train at South Kensington and seated himself happily in the front carriage anticipating his arrival at what would be the terminus. He returned home much later in a state of shock, withdrawn and tearful. Few people used the tube in the afternoon in those days and the small boy had been paralysed with fear when he was approached by a man and severely molested. Julian remembers: 'I had been told nothing about sex, so I was completely floored by what happened.' It was a traumatic experience that left a black mark. From being an outgoing, happy child he became nervous and shy overnight. Looking back on the incident he feels strongly that his parents were to blame and should never have allowed him to make all those journeys alone.

Nevertheless, that same year, Julian and Andrew both won Junior Exhibitioner scholarships to attend the Saturday morning sessions at the Royal College of Music. This was an exciting new venture for the brothers and, when Julian was put in the care of Rhuna Martin for his cello lessons, he really began to enjoy his playing – he found that she was the sort of teacher to whom he could respond. 'Rhuna talked about *music* not technique, and that was what I wanted to hear. We got stuck into major cello music – Bruch's *Kol Nidrei* and the Brahms E minor Sonata – doubtless far too soon, but I loved it. She also took me to hear the first great cellist I ever heard – Pierre Fournier. I was transfixed. I didn't believe it was possible to play the cello that way. I told her I would never play like that, but she simply said: "You will." Of course I never believed her, but it was nice to feel that the person who watched, listened and guided me each week felt such confidence in me – she was giving me the encouragement I needed.'

Today, Rhuna Martin remembers very well her lessons with the ten-year-old: 'He was a lovely little boy, and I recognised at once that he was not only gifted musically, but also very bright. He seemed to understand exactly what I was trying to teach him and he would grasp an idea immediately.'

Another aspect of the Junior College sessions, which was soon to have enormous repercussions for the Lloyd Webber family, was that everyone was expected to take up a second instrument. A performance of Haydn's Military Symphony was scheduled by the College orchestra so both Andrew and Julian decided to opt for the percussion section – Andrew on the cymbals and Julian on the bass drum, or *Gran Cassa* as it was called on the orchestral parts. This necessitated a great deal of home practice, which would have done little to help Carleton Hobbs' concentration on his Sherlock Holmes scripts.

This sudden involvement with the orchestral percussion brought the boys into contact with a fellow student who was destined to play a huge part in their lives, the pianist John Lill. He was then sixteen and later to be the winner of the world's most prestigious piano prize – the International Tchaikovsky Piano Competition in Moscow. John was playing timpani in the orchestra and according to Julian was 'quite the loudest drummer' he had ever heard. John later went on to play in the College's Senior Orchestra and Julian says he had it on good authority that after the immense drum-roll in the first movement of Beethoven's Choral Symphony – usually played by a relay of timpanists but which John did on his own – the entire brass section, who were sitting only a few inches in front, were deafened for a week!

John Lill remembers very well that he suddenly became aware of this 'delightful little boy' with an endearing smile sitting in the timps section, observing everything he was doing: 'One day he came over to me and said in a high, squeaky voice: "My mother would like to invite you to lunch."'

John Lill came from a poor working-class background in the East End of London and when he followed up the invitation into this eccentric family it was an experience he will never forget: 'It was very strange coming into the comparative opulence of Harrington Court. The family were all very unusual, to say the least, and this I liked, since I tend to prefer individuals to run-of-the-mill people. I soon became a regular visitor and I cannot describe their kindness and generosity towards me over many years.'

Jean immediately recognised John Lill's talent and took possession of him as her prodigy from the first day they met. For John, this was 'a gift from God' and eventually, Lill felt almost part of the Lloyd Webber family. On reflection, he feels that at the time it must have been very difficult for his own mother to accept, especially as she saw so little of him during the formative years when his career as a soloist was developing. It was through Jean that he achieved his London début playing Rachmaninov's Third Piano Concerto at the Royal College with Sir Adrian Boult conducting. Lill acknowledges that over the years she did all she could, not only for him but for many others. However, he does admit that she became over-possessive – which did not have a good effect on Andrew in particular. Andrew always felt that his mother showed more interest in John than in him and resented all the attention she bestowed upon the interloper. Julian, being that much younger, does not recall feeling any such jealousy. Curiously, he feels that any resentment he might have had towards John joining the household was because Andrew now seemed to enjoy a companionship with John that he had only previously shared with his younger brother.

John and Julian are good friends and colleagues today, yet there was an early occasion when disaster struck the relationship. Julian's progress had been duly noted by the powers that be and he was invited to perform a solo at one of their end-of-term concerts. It was a great opportunity and he managed to persuade John to accompany him. It was decided he should play the *Tarantella* by Squire, a very fast piece with a lengthy piano introduction. The description of what happened is best told in Julian's own words: 'The dignified Royal College concert hall was packed with people who had come to see their star pianist accompany this dreadful little boy in short trousers, but unfortunately the whole thing proved too much for me – with catastrophic results. In the heat of the moment I was convinced John had started off much too fast and after a few bars I stopped, swung round to the piano and cried in a loud squeaky voice: "Start again, it's too fast!" John had no alternative, and so, with a look on his face that would have frozen the Equator solid and to the vast amusement of the entire audience, the future Tchaikovsky competition winner was forced to begin all over again at an altogether statelier pace. The piece ended to tumultuous applause but John was never allowed to live that episode down. To this day, when he proudly boasts never to have stopped during one of his concerts, there's always someone who'll pipe up: "But don't you remember the Squire *Tarantella*?"'

On Saturday afternoons, when College was finished, Jean Lloyd Webber would drive John home and call on his mother with Julian in tow. While the two women 'gossiped', Julian would go to watch football down the road at Leyton Orient. Julian recalls: 'The "Os" were then in the First Division (now the Premier League) and they actually beat Liverpool and Manchester United that season.' Julian remains furiously jealous that John Lill actually saw the match when Orient gained promotion to this exalted company for the one and only season in their history, especially as John has no interest in football whatsoever and only went to this momentous match because it seemed to encompass the entire population of Leyton.

Today, Lill loves to tell a story involving his father, the Orient and Julian. John's father, who worked at the nearby metal works, also drew cartoons for the local paper. This entitled him to a press pass for all Orient's home games. When one vital fixture was completely sold out, Julian begged John's dad to take him along too, but Lill senior had only one seat. So the pair went off to the match and were only allowed in when Lill concocted a story that the little boy was his son and would sit on his lap. Unfortunately, they were only just through the turnstile when Julian swung round to John's father and exclaimed in a loud, squeaky voice: 'Thank you so much, Mr Lill!'

From his first visit to Leyton Orient, Julian would watch them lose, week after week, and he feels sure that it must be his underlying sympathy for the underdog that inspired him to become a true supporter. Today he remains just as fanatical about the 'Os' as he was as an eleven-year-old: whenever his concert schedule permits he will be found at Brisbane Road – a perverse example, perhaps, of Julian's extreme loyalty to causes, and even people, who are dear to him.

When Junior College was nearing its end for Julian, Rhuna Martin felt that that he was now ready for a teacher who could take him to another dimension. There was also another more domestic reason. Rhuna had visited Harrington Court on many occasions and saw that it was – to say the least – an unconventional background. She was quite terrified of Molly – who was doubtless very soft underneath but 'presented a formidable appearance'. She also had her doubts about Jean. Rhuna knew that she was supportive of everything her sons undertook, but at the same time she recognised an enormous strength of will and felt that the small boy was being overpowered by two very strong women. 'What Julian needed was some male influence and I thought that Douglas Cameron would be just the right person.'

Although Julian now enjoyed playing his cello, when one summer holiday his parents insisted that he take it with him to practise he decided that this was a step too far. Unfortunately, they were not to be dissuaded so he devised a plan to render his cello unplayable by way of a 'terrible accident'. He took his bow, cracked it across his knee and immediately rushed to show it to his mother saying: 'Look what's happened. I didn't realise it was there and I sat on it.' There followed an awful silence when he realised that he was just as shocked as she was. But he could tell from her face that she could not possibly imagine that her little boy had done something quite so dreadful on purpose. Julian's extra enjoyment of the holiday was only slightly tinged with shame, which soon disappeared when the bow was returned from the repairer with hardly a sign of the mishap. He still has that bow and even uses it from time to time. But he never takes it on holiday.

The cacophonous household on the top floor continued to resound with Andrew's piano and horn (a recent addition to his accomplishments), Julian's cello and trumpet (another new aural embellishment) and Jean, Bill and John's pianos – at one point they owned at least three. All this, along with Bill's electric organ and Molly's deafening TV finally proved too much even for the saintly Carleton Hobbs. At long last he complained: once, when Julian dropped a load of bricks on the floor and again when Andrew's stomping on the floor to beat time proved too much for his ceiling and it descended to the middle of his sitting room carpet.

At the age of ten, nothing was further from Julian's mind than taking up music as a profession. He loved playing the cello but it was mainly for fun and he had never practised properly, even though he managed to scrape through all his Associated Board exams. At the time, musically he felt close to his brother who used to bring home all the latest hit records from Bill Haley, Elvis and his own favourite of the time, Bobby Vee.

But Julian was increasingly drawn to music written for the cello. The *Radio Times* used to list music broadcasts from foreign radio stations, and he would scan it each week in the hope of catching an unknown cello concerto by an equally unknown composer. He discovered concertos by people like Pipkov and Dukelsky and recorded them all – intermittent cracklings and splutterings permitting – on his old reel-to-reel tape recorder. He soon built up an enormous collection, which he still possesses: 'while other little boys collected cigarette cards, I was collecting obscure cello concertos!'

Julian continued to take every opportunity to hear cellists in London, but still had no intention of entering the music profession himself. In December 1963, at the age of twelve, he had an experience that had a cataclysmic effect on his entire attitude towards the cello and his future in music. It was hearing the great Russian cellist Rostropovich for the first time in concert. Eighteen months later, Rostropovich gave a series of nine concerts with the London Symphony Orchestra that claimed to present the complete repertoire for cello and orchestra. Julian went to each one but, even in those early days, was put out by the fact that the concertos by Delius, Walton and Khachaturian were missing. Nonetheless, the concerts proved a turning point. No other performer had ever made that kind of impact on him and Rostropovich's programme note sounded a particular resonance: 'The cello,' wrote Rostopovich, 'without losing its power to express lyrical emotions and moods, has become in our times a tribune, an orator, a dramatic hero.' Julian knew that Rostropovich was acting as an ambassador for the cello and it struck an immediate chord in his imagination.

Today, Julian is still convinced that Rostropovich remains a unique cellist: 'Over the years I have heard many cellists and can always follow what they are doing on the instrument. In other words, I realise that whatever technique they use, it is possible and recognisable. But Rostropovich in his prime would do things that I couldn't understand, that I couldn't explain. *That* is genius.'

No account of life at No. 10 would be complete without mention of *the cats*. The whole family loved cats and Jean was so besotted with them that she treated them better than humans. Bill owned a beautiful Siamese called Perseus who spent most of the time perched on his shoulder rather like Long John Silver's parrot in *Treasure Island*. When Perseus died, the whole family went into mourning. Years later, when recalling the incident, Jean said that he had such a personality that it seemed impossible to contemplate life without him. In fact, Bill was so distressed that he announced they would never again have another cat. Jean said nothing but remembered thinking she would rather have a cat than be cat-less and, sure enough, within days, Sergei (Prokoviev), a Russian Blue, and Dimitry (Shostakovich), another Siamese, had been added to the fold.

Julian was now hard at work with his new teacher Douglas Cameron – known to everyone as 'Douggie'. Cameron was responsible for teaching an entire generation of British cellists, including the principals of three of the four London orchestras, Keith Harvey, Christopher Van Kampen, and Douglas Cummings. He also founded a cello club in London where he managed to persuade many of the world's leading cellists to come and play without a fee – no small achievement! Among those who obliged were Rostropovich, Paul Tortelier and Sir John Barbirolli.

A short, stout, red-faced Scot, Douggie was a great character universally loved in the music profession and, as Julian once remarked: 'To say that Douggie liked a drink would be the musical understatement of the century.' Many people who knew him and were aware of his constant tippling wondered how he ever managed to obtain such good results from his students. According to Julian, the trick was to make sure that lessons were first thing in the morning when the previous night's excesses had worn off and the new day's had not quite begun.

Once, when Julian made the mistake of fixing a lesson for the afternoon, he arrived at Douggie's house with some trepidation at about 3pm but there was no reply. 'Eventually, after repeated ringings, Douggie lurched to the door and let me in. He was in a terrible state, for apparently his previous pupil had asked him straight out whether he thought he was good enough to make it as a soloist and, having had even more whisky than usual, had said he didn't think so. I said I thought he had done the kindest thing, but Douggie obviously felt very bad about it and there was a terrible atmosphere of depression. Considerably more whisky flowed throughout my "lesson" during which he fell asleep, woke up with a start, called me Gayle (the name of a delightful blonde girl he was teaching at the time) and dozed off to sleep again. Eventually I gave up, packed the cello and crept out of the house.'

Despite these occasional lapses, Cameron was a remarkable teacher, loved and respected by his students. Even today, Julian regards him as the teacher who exerted the greatest influence on him. His approach was based on the idea of bringing out the best in each individual rather than imposing a particular style. On one occasion, Paul Tortelier – well known for his master classes on television – went to judge a competition at the Royal Academy where Cameron was professor. Tortelier was interested to know who the competitors' different teachers were, as they played with such individuality. He could hardly believe it when he was told that they were all with the same professor.

Julian believes the quality that made Cameron such an outstanding teacher was his lack of conceit. He never suggested his pupils should copy him and would find some encouraging remark even for the least talented of his students. Looking back Julian feels that this is perhaps what he appreciated most: 'I was never very responsive to the kind of teacher who is musically dogmatic – or dogmatic in any respect. My own approach to each piece was so conscientious and painstaking that if I came up against somebody else who took the same careful attitude and it wasn't the same as mine, I couldn't go along with it. I always responded better to the teacher who would let me do my own thing but at the same time knocked off all the rough edges.'

So it was, spurred on by the example of Rostropovich and the inspiration of Douglas Cameron, that Julian knew, at the age of thirteen, that there was nothing else he could do. He had to become a solo cellist.

Chapter 3

The Searching Years

Having made his decision, Julian never wavered. Even at thirteen he was determined never to become an orchestral player – no taking orders from all those conductors! He would be a solo cellist or nothing. But this was easier said than done. He clearly had a talent but, because he had never practised in an organised way, his playing, technically, lagged behind that of his contemporaries.

He soon discovered it was considered an almost impossible task to become a solo cellist. Even Douglas Cameron knew from long experience that so many of his pupils had started out with great ambitions only to end up sad and disillusioned. Julian also remembered his father's advice never to enter the music profession *'unless there is nothing else you can do'*.

His father had made it very clear that music is a tough profession and that only those who are prepared to fight against all odds are likely to succeed. But, typically, the more Julian was told it was impossible, the more determined he became. With Rostropovich as his role model, it was a challenge that he was ready to accept. One day he would show these fainthearted detractors that he would win.

It was this perhaps naïve but persistent attitude that helped him through when all he would hear was: 'Sorry, there's no demand for solo cellists'. Unlike his father, rejection made Julian even more determined: 'I think Douglas Cameron must have been surprised at my change in attitude during my first lessons with him. Although still at school I would rush home and practise with real enthusiasm for the first time.' He feels certain that his school friends must have found him rather odd because suddenly he was no longer interested in going with them to films or parties (it was, after all, the 'swinging sixties') but stayed at home voluntarily to practise.

As his lessons with Cameron continued Julian became more and more adventurous in his choice of repertoire: 'When Douggie suggested that I learned the Shostakovich Sonata, I insisted on tackling the much harder Concerto instead. He said I wasn't ready for it. I asked him to let me bring both pieces the next week and he could judge for himself. Not surprisingly, I made sure he let me get on with the Concerto.'

From thirteen to sixteen Julian attended University College School in Hampstead. In those days, it could hardly be called a musical school as the music teacher doubled as the gym master! Nonetheless, Julian's talent was recognised by an anonymous contributor to the school magazine reporting on a concert given on Speech Day 1967: 'If one had to pick a highlight... the following item would be the most likely choice. This was the Allegretto from the Cello Concerto No. 1 by Shostakovich played by Lloyd Webber, cello, and Katz, piano (orchestral reduction). The cellist displayed a truly virtuoso technique, performing throughout with a panache rarely found among school musicians.'[4]

Once again, the inclusion of this work in his repertoire paid off handsomely, when that same year he won scholarships to both the Royal College and the Royal Academy, playing the Shostakovich and Boccherini concertos on each occasion. However, he did not take up either scholarship for another year as he felt he wanted a really intensive period of study with Cameron.

Julian's decision to leave school at sixteen meant that he did not have an impressive academic record. He had only five 'O' Levels and his school reports were not too encouraging. This did not seem to bother his parents unduly. In fact it is on record that when one report was particularly damning, Jean became convulsed with laughter.

Nonetheless, underneath Julian's ambition to become a soloist there was a deep-rooted sense of insecurity. On one hand, he thought he could overcome the obstacles if he tried hard enough, but on the other there was always the question of whether he had the talent and could earn a living. He frequently imagined himself working in a supermarket or being on the street with no money at all. These were frightening thoughts for a teenager, especially as he never confided them to anyone else.

When it came to taking up his scholarship, he was faced with a difficult decision: 'If I had chosen to go to the academy I would almost certainly have been put with Douggie, who was the chief professor there, and from whom I'd already learned a tremendous amount. But, if I went to the college where my father had been a professor for years, I would have the opportunity of a change of teacher and of experiencing a different approach. I chose the college – not because I thought I had learned all I could from Douggie, but because I thought I might benefit from the change.'

At the Royal College, Julian experienced quite a different approach under Joan Dickson, and for a time with Harvey Phillips. Later, he regretted not having worked more intensively with Cameron. Most of his lessons had been when Julian was still at school and with hindsight he realised there was so much music that he would have liked to have covered with him. Julian made up for this by regularly playing pieces to Cameron until his death in 1974.

Just before he entered the college, in May 1968, Julian gave what was to be the last concert under Cameron's tuition. It was a family affair at the Central Hall, Westminster, where William Lloyd Webber was organist. Andrew had written a piece with his new lyricist Tim Rice, based on the Bible story of Joseph and his coat of many colours. It had been a success at Colet Court boys' school (the preparatory for St Paul's) and it was decided to give it a public airing. A concert was arranged in aid of the new drug-addiction centre that had recently been set up at Central Hall. John Lill played piano, Bill played the organ and it was advertised as the première of *Joseph and the Amazing Technicolour Dreamcoat*. In addition, Julian was to play the Saint-Saëns Cello Concerto, accompanied by his father on the piano.

There was a great deal of interest in the event and on the night the hall was packed with an audience of almost three thousand. Julian had never played to such a vast number of people and he became almost paralysed with nerves. He says: 'I thought I had played unbelievably badly and my first concert review in a national newspaper resulted in my first disagreement with a critic. Meirion Bowen in *The Times* declared it "a superb account of the concerto."'[5]

After the concert, Julian was thoroughly depressed and beat a hasty retreat through the back door. It was here he encountered his very first fan. She was an attractive blonde girl of about sixteen who handed him her autograph book and said, giggling: 'You were brilliant.' It cheered him up no end and he thanked her profusely for the first ever request for his autograph. They chatted awkwardly for a few moments and then went their separate ways but, six years later, Celia Ballantyne would become his wife. She remembers the occasion as though it were yesterday: 'His composure on the platform was amazing for a seventeen-year-old. There is one place towards the end of the concerto where there is an ascending scale that ends up in harmonics. In the middle of this passage the spike of his cello slipped across the floor but Julian handled it like a veteran, and didn't bat an eyelid.'

Celia Ballantyne was born in Walton-on-Thames, the daughter of a doctor who had come from a family of music lovers. His mother was an artist who had played the cello and her three children had all inherited some artistic gift. Celia had started learning the cello at the age of five, studying with Elizabeth Hewlins, co-founder of the enterprising Pro Corda – who organised holiday chamber music courses for youngsters at Leiston Abbey in Suffolk. Celia continued her lessons until she was thirteen but decided that she would never make the grade as a musician.

Celia's first contact with the Lloyd Webbers had been through her elder brother David, who was in the pop music business. She remembers first meeting Andrew and Tim Rice at a party in Kew when she was about fifteen. Apparently, Julian was also there with a group of friends but they did not meet. The first time she heard him play was at the Central Hall concert. Then, in 1969, she and her brother were invited to Andrew's 21st birthday party, and this time she was not only introduced to Julian, but made an impression on him that he was unlikely to forget. She had had a few too many drinks, felt considerably worse for wear and Julian took it upon himself to look after her. Shortly after this she heard again from her new benefactor: 'I remember so well that he sent me a telegram – as we were not on the phone – and it simply said "Please ring Kensington 8614", so I went down to the phone box at the end of the road, dialled the number, pressed Button A and put my four pennies in. Julian asked me if I would like to go to a concert on 29 April at the Royal Festival Hall when Tortelier was playing. I said yes, and that was it.'

By now, the family at 10 Harrington Court had acquired so many satellite members that more room was urgently needed and Molly managed to rent the flat next door – No. 2a – which was joined to No. 10 by a balcony above the street. Despite her deafness, even *she* was finding the accumulated sounds of the sundry instruments at No. 10 somewhat overpowering. She moved into No. 2a along with John Lill and Tim Rice – Andrew's newly acquired lyricist – who paid the Lloyd Webbers £5 a week for the privilege of his London 'pad'. They made a most unusual threesome. Lill recalls: 'Tim had a stream of attractive girlfriends who constantly floated in and out at all hours in various stages of undress'. Tim Rice's initial impression was nothing like the 'well-ordered rule' of his own childhood: 'I was part of a free-range if not deranged set-up with a fascinatingly wacky cast of enchanting characters. This suited me fine. Andrew seemed to rule the roost, with an ability to summon almost any member of the family to do his bidding, mainly his devoted gran. Now and then I caught a hint of the odd flare-up from a distance but was usually able to lie low until the all-clear was sounded.'

He was also very fond of Molly: 'She subscribed to the laissez-faire ambience of the household, seeming far less shocked than I was by the four-letter words, and by the total lack of respect for things held sacred in my parents' home, such as school reports, table-manners and parents themselves. Yet the chaos engendered, at least as far as I could tell, a happy, as well as an extraordinarily noisy, atmosphere.'[6]

In 1967 Andrew had been awarded an exhibition at Magdalen College, Oxford, but stayed for just one term because he soon realised that 'classics' were not his *métier*. Jean was furious at him for giving up such an opportunity in order to write musicals. Bill took a more liberal view – he was all for his sons deciding what they wanted to do for themselves. But Andrew's return to the fold presented problems for Julian. Andrew was now composing continuously on the piano accompanied by fierce foot-stamping on the pedal. With the added sounds of Lill's piano and Bill's electric organ, it is not difficult to imagine Julian's struggle to concentrate as he attempted to practise his cello.

Now that he had taken the decision to become a soloist,

Julian was obsessive about practising and, as every other room seemed to be occupied, he was obliged to use the main sitting room opening on to the balcony which connected the two flats. He recalled an endless stream of people walking to and fro with what seemed to be the sole object of interrupting his playing. At the same time, Andrew would play pop music at an ear-splitting level on the solitary turntable, while Julian only wanted to hear Rostropovich or Casals. In the past, apart from the normal sibling rivalry, they had managed to tolerate each other. But now there was open warfare. They had heated arguments that usually ended with Andrew screaming and threatening to leave; but since he had nowhere to go, he too felt even more frustrated. They would finally make it up but as soon as Andrew's foot-stamping recommenced, yet another battle would ensue.

Often, when John Lill was away Julian would seize the opportunity to practise in his bedroom in No. 2a. But the incessant sound of the cello annoyed a young neighbour from the flat below, who eventually came up to complain. By this time, Julian had gone back to No. 10 and it was Tim Rice who opened the door.

'That noise,' the neighbour moaned, 'that bloody oboe thing.'

'Yes, that bloody oboe thing.'

'Can't you stop it? Just for a day?' Tim Rice promised he would. When Julian returned later Tim enquired gleefully: 'How's the oboe?'

'The what?'

'You know, the bloody oboe thing.'

From this point on, 'How's the oboe?' became a familiar taunt and is still something that Tim Rice never lets Julian forget.

In 1968 when Julian entered the Royal College it was the tail-end of the 'swinging sixties' when London was *the* place to be and parties were the order of the day. If the truth be told, work came a poor second for many of the students, who mostly seemed to spend their time in Room 99 (their nickname for the pub around the corner). The college originally had 98 rooms and when a new wing was eventually added, its room numbers tactfully started at 100.

Apart from the fact that they were both cellists, the only other thing Julian's new professor, Joan Dickson, had in common with Douglas Cameron was that they were both Scots. She certainly did not share Douggie's taste for whisky and her strict method of teaching contrasted greatly with Cameron's relaxed style. Although Julian did not fully appreciate it at the time, Dickson's disciplined approach had a lasting effect on him and they covered a great deal of music in their two years together. Many of her lessons were in the form of 'master-classes' – which, in the wrong hands, can be an ego-trip for the professor in charge. The unassuming and modest Joan Dickson could never have been accused of that. She preferred to call her classes 'workshops' and other cellists were the only people encouraged to attend. But Julian found 'other cellists' the worst possible audience: 'My left-hand fingers would sweat. I would slide to all the wrong notes and my concentration would disappear completely.' Worst of all, his right hand would begin to shake, causing the bow to bounce on the strings – a malady known in the profession as 'the pearlies'. The more he tried to stop the shaking, the worse it became until, one day, he dropped the bow altogether.

What Julian did not realise was that this 'experience' was the best possible preparation for the concert platform as he was forced to find ways of controlling his nerves. He discovered that 'you have to lose yourself totally in the music so that the body becomes a channel through which it can flow. If the mind is given over completely to something outside the physical body, nerves disappear. Although part of the mind has to be aware of its physical surroundings, the technical side of a performance should have been prepared before, so leaving the music to take control.'

This condition can only be practised by performance itself, which in turn increases confidence. There were days when his nervousness seemed to be uncontrollable and, in time, Julian learnt one or two specific ways to deal with the problem: 'When my right hand began shaking and the bow bounced all over the strings I would immediately focus attention on my left-hand fingerings – I'd forget about the bow and it would start to behave properly again.' As for nerves before a concert he believes that they can be made to work *for*, rather than against you because the extra flow of adrenalin sharpens the reflexes and gives each performance a special edge.

If classes were a problem for Julian, orchestra was far worse. A few days after his arrival Julian discovered he had been made leader of the cello section, which meant that frequently a solo would be required. Cocooned by the sound of the orchestra all around him, Julian would suddenly spot the word 'Solo' and realise that all too soon the rest of the cello section would lapse into silence and he would find himself alone. He readily remembers the terror that struck even though it was so many years ago: 'The audience aren't expecting you to play by yourself and when it happens you can feel their eyes swivel in your direction with surprise and anticipation. It is a truly terrible moment.'

However, there are compensations in orchestral playing, as Julian soon discovered, for the companionship that exists among the members is never possible for a soloist. This cama-raderie was brought home to him at the end of his first year at college. Julian was one of a group of students who were hand-picked by a certain conductor to tour Austria as a 'baroque' ensemble during the summer vacation – all expenses paid.

Musically, the trip was a disaster. The conductor was hesitant and his beat was a miracle of indecision. Every performance had its casualties, which resulted either in cacophony or an unexpected silence, which – in one concert – was interrupted by a trumpeter who came in fortissimo all by himself. Afterwards, many of the orchestra were in tears. 'Finally we decided the only way of getting to the end of each concert was to play the pieces ourselves and totally ignore any further directions from the crazed conductor – who by this time had resolved to give up music altogether as soon as he got home.' It was Julian's first experience of what is known in the profession as 'automatic pilot.'

However, playing in the college orchestra did have its lighter moments. On one occasion a 'distinguished' composer from a leading German university was invited as a visiting professor and it was decided that the orchestra would benefit from playing his latest 'masterpiece'. 'Unfortunately, the mass of squiggles, arrows and circles on the page seemed to defy any kind of rational explanation and the professor's vain attempts to enlighten us, in faltering English, only made things worse.' One sign apparently meant that they were to bash the side of the instrument with the left hand while bowing on the wrong side of the bridge with the other. 'Accompanied as we were by a drum we must have sounded like a pack of wolves on heat!' This naturally caused much merriment among the orchestra, which, sadly, was not shared by the professor, who by this time was in a foul temper.

Things were made considerably worse when in the middle of one dirge-like passage on the depths of the C string a voice from the back grumbled:'It sounds like an incontinent fly.'

This was too much. The entire cello section doubled up over their instruments in uncontrollable laughter and the apoplectic German flung his baton to the ground in disgust. Julian, as leader of the section, had to bear the brunt of his wrath...

'Dass iss ze musik off ze future!' he boomed. 'You vil not blame me ven you haff to play ziz and do not know how should go!'

Roused by the indignation at what he had been forced to inflict upon his long-suffering cello all afternoon, Julian shouted that he would rather starve than play his so-called 'music.' Feeling that there was no point in staying around any longer he stormed off the platform followed by a retinue of fellow cellists – 'a magnificent victory for the Cellists' Liberation Front,' Julian later remarked.

Doubtless, all these experiences were good training for a future in music and Julian looks back on his time at the college as being of the greatest value. He disagrees with the modern idea that an aspiring soloist is far better taking a year off to study with some great 'name' abroad. He also disagrees with the late Sir Thomas Beecham, who declared that Benjamin Britten was 'the only worthwhile English composer to have emanated from one of our colleges of music.' Julian asks: 'What about Holst or Vaughan Williams?' For him, the 'year's study abroad' – which many find obligatory – can be simply another way of putting off the inevitable moment of truth on the concert platform. He considers that no amount of lessons can be a substitute for the real experience of giving concerts and feels that the longer the début is postponed, the more difficult it will be to confront an audience. He maintains that, in any case, however successful one may become, there is always more work to be done, so the learning process never finishes. Usually, when a student has completed his or her time at college, they take an associate diploma either in performing or in teaching. Julian had taken his performer's diploma in the autumn *before* he started college, which meant that he had no specific academic goal to reach there and was always aiming at the musical world beyond.

In 1970, John Lill won the world's top piano prize – the International Tchaikovsky Competition in Moscow. Everyone at Harrington Court was overjoyed. Suddenly, Lill found himself booked for concerts all over the world, but it was one at the Royal Hall, Harrogate, in aid of Oxfam, that Julian remembers most vividly. The programme was a celebration of Beethoven's bi-centenary and consisted of Beethoven piano sonatas, but for one item, John had invited his young cellist friend to join him. The critic from the *Yorkshire Post* commented: 'John Lill joined with a yet younger colleague, Julian Lloyd Webber, in a performance of Beethoven's D major sonata for cello and piano that suggested not only a meeting of minds but also the arrival of an extremely fine cello player. The calmness of the slow movement was absolute and the fugue, far from being a struggle to be heard, was a well-balanced interplay between the instruments, in turns piquant and forceful but always incisive.'[7]

Harrogate was a beginning but Julian knew that it would be essential to have concert dates in his diary by the time he left college. (His father had left him in no doubt that he would not be providing any 'hand-outs'.) Julian therefore decided to make his London début recital with the pianist Clifford Benson at the Wigmore Hall while still a student in the hope that he would receive good reviews that would give him his first step on the ladder. It was in December 1971 and Julian clearly remembers how he felt before that momentous occasion: 'Nothing can ever quite equal the crescendo of excitement before your first "official" public concert. This is the moment when you have to prove you can do it, the moment when all the talk, the scholarships and the student success count for nothing. In London you play to one of the world's most sophisticated audiences, so used to their glittering array of passing musical stars that they almost take them for granted.' He chose his programme with care but with an audacity that frightens him today. It frightened him then too, but he wanted to show he could interpret the classic sonatas of Beethoven and Brahms as well as some British music. So between the final Beethoven D major and the Brahms F major he played the Delius Sonata. He could not sleep afterwards and kept going over the concert again and again wondering if he could have done better. Then there was the terrifying prospect of the next day's newspapers. When they arrived, Julian could not bear to look so his mother read from the *Daily Telegraph:* 'An exceptional talent, the 20-year-old cellist Julian Lloyd Webber made his first Wigmore Hall sonata recital last night a very distinguished affair...the rich adagio and the athletic fugue of Beethoven's Sonata in D major were marvellously integrated and balanced...An expansive account of the Delius Sonata brought out the opulence of the instrument.' Julian glowed with sheer delight and picked up the paper to read for himself. He then spotted the heading that had obviously been devised by an overnight sub editor who was probably feeling a little weary and ready for his bed. It proclaimed: *An exceptional talent at the piano.*[8]

There was some consolation a week later when *The Times* critic wrote: 'Mr Lloyd Webber's cello tone is full and clear, his control assured: this combination worked like a dream in the nostalgic effusion of Delius's Sonata.'[9]

Julian auditioned for two further London concerts and one for a series for young artists on Dutch television. He also entered a competition administered by the Philharmonia Orchestra to take lessons from the great French cellist Pierre Fournier. If this was successful he realised he could combine concerts with some further study. He won all four competitions and everything else went according to plan. He could now look with some confidence to the future.

However, it was the college itself that presented Julian with his first big break. He had auditioned for their 'Concerto Trials' to perform the long and extremely difficult *Sinfonia Concertante* by Prokofiev and was chosen to play the work in a special eightieth birthday celebration for the Master of the Queen's Musick, Sir Arthur Bliss. After the concert was over, Sir Arthur left a parcel for him with Sir Keith Falkner, the College Director. Julian opened it with trembling fingers and could hardly believe his eyes. It was an inscribed score of the composer's own Cello Concerto.

Julian knew that it had recently been premièred by his hero, Rostropovich, at the Aldeburgh Festival and he was delighted at the prospect of learning it during the summer holidays. When he felt he was ready, he wrote to Sir Arthur asking if he could come and play it through to him, although he feared that the composer would have forgotten all about him. The following morning, the phone rang and he was amazed to hear the very young and lively sounding voice of Sir Arthur Bliss asking if he could come to play the concerto to him later that week. With fear and trepidation Julian went along to his house in St. John's Wood – having hurriedly organised for someone to play the orchestral part on the piano. It was the first time he had ever played a work through to its composer and he was convinced that Sir Arthur was bound to be the most severe critic. He was wrong.

Sir Arthur seemed pleased that he had learned it from memory, but this apart, he hardly made any comment at all. Julian thought that Bliss had probably disliked his performance so did not see any point in discussing it further. The young cellist left feeling thoroughly depressed. He had enjoyed working on the concerto but now it all seemed to have been a complete waste of time.

A few days later, the new college year was due to begin and Julian was obliged to attend his usual annual speech. Still in a mood of deep depression his musings were suddenly interrupted by Sir Keith saying: '...and Julian played it "like the British Rostropovich".'

Julian's confidence received a further boost when Ronald Crichton reviewed the college concert in the *Financial Times*: 'Bliss was paired with his contemporary, Prokofiev. The long, not very coherent, but often tuneful and colourful *Sinfonia Concertante* for cello and orchestra was given a remarkable performance by Julian Lloyd Webber, who had the work by heart. Ideally, it needs firmer definition to hold it together, but to ask for this as well in a score that eludes total success even in the grandest professional performances would be unreasonable.'[10]

When the full story of the Director's meeting with Sir Arthur emerged, Julian was stunned. It seems that the composer had done nothing but enthuse over Julian's playing and had gone to the extent of suggesting he give the first London performance the following year at the Queen Elizabeth Hall. This was the première that was to launch Julian's career, thanks to the Prokofiev at the Royal College.

This first important break into the concert world would never have come about if Julian had completed his studies abroad. He feels strongly about the mistaken attitude that music colleges do nothing to help students obtain engagements: 'Perhaps there is some truth in this view since inevitably the vast majority of students will either become orchestral players or teachers. Perhaps the college system is not geared to producing soloists. I would personally like to see one music college that concentrates entirely upon performing. At the moment, they all run teachers' courses. But the Royal College gave me the opportunity to play an important concerto while I was still a student. It was my first big "break".'

Another legendary figure who had happened to attend that fateful college concert was Mrs Emmie Tillett of Ibbs & Tillett Ltd, one of the most important concert agencies in the world at that time. Almost every great name imaginable had at some time been managed by 'Ibbs'. Emmie was a formidable businesswoman with a charming personality, but she was also extremely shrewd. When she sent a date and time for an interview – it was more of a command – he could not hesitate. Julian felt very strange sitting in her office surrounded by scores of signed photographs of legendary artists from Casals to Rachmaninov, but the meeting was highly successful. She had been impressed by his playing and offered him management starting from the time when he left college in the summer of 1972. He still had a year to go and he already had an agent. Life was looking rosier by the day.

Chapter 4

Life Without Molly

Molly died in 1971 but little changed at Harrington Court except that now Jean, somewhat reluctantly, had to take on the domestic side of things. However, she still spent most of her time teaching and on her charitable causes while keeping an obsessive watch on her prodigy, John Lill, who was now well on the way to the top. Bill, meanwhile, in addition to his appointments at Central Hall Westminster and the Royal College of Music, had taken on the directorship of the London College of Music in 1961. Doubtless he felt obliged to earn a regular income (he had, after all, a wife and two children to feed) but this addition to his academic duties was perhaps his final admittance of defeat as a composer. He now regarded himself as a complete failure and his depression, which had led to heavy drinking, was becoming a major problem. He could not accept what he saw as the injustice of the situation yet, in common with all pessimists, he would make no effort to promote himself, so it was very difficult to help him. Whenever anyone had the temerity to suggest he was being unduly pessimistic and should persevere with sending his work to publishers, he would insist, 'I'm am not a pessimist; I am just being realistic,' so the argument would end and his music would remain stuffed in a drawer.

In his solitude Bill would suffer the pain he could not show to the outside world. Julian remembers only too well waking several times in the middle of the night to discover his father listening to an old acetate recording of the first performance of his *Aurora*, and sobbing like a small child. Julian never told anyone, even in the family. He says, 'I remember so well hearing this music which I thought was incredibly beautiful – but his composing was never talked about at home. It was more or less a taboo subject.' Nonetheless, the atmosphere at Harrington Court had a deep psychological effect upon Julian's – and most likely Andrew's – attitude towards fulfilling talent and ambition and even towards the consumption of alcohol (Julian will only drink beer). Bill's alcoholism began in the mid-sixties and, by the early seventies, had reached the point where he would start drinking in the morning and was almost always drunk by the evening. Julian remembers his little table that stood in the hall where he would mix the most unbelievably potent cocktails in a large jug. When the contents had been transferred to another for easy pouring, he would fill the original one with water. When visitors arrived he would offer them a drink, and – if they asked for water – he would pour it from this jug. Soon afterwards, they would stagger out, having consumed the most alcoholic glass of water they would ever taste. Attempts by the family to stop him proved useless. The main problem was the usual one. He refused to admit he was an alcoholic so nothing would persuade him that he needed help. Once, when his doctor finally told him that his drinking was affecting his chances of survival, he went 'on the wagon' for a few days. He stopped his alcohol intake immediately and drank masses of tomato juice only to be admitted as an emergency patient at the local hospital with acute tomato juice poisoning! This was the limit of his 'abstinence' and he was soon back to his normal drinking habit. Yet, surprisingly, when his doctor had made a similar threat about his heavy smoking, he also stopped overnight but he never returned to the habit.

Bill's problems were deeply rooted in his childhood. Although his father was extremely proud of him, once Bill became a professional musician, he felt he could no longer communicate with him on the same level, simply because his son had 'outgrown' him. So, Bill had to make his own way. Later, Bill apparently felt the same way about Andrew and Julian. He firmly believed that when talent is handed down from one generation to the next, each generation develops it as far as possible, then the next takes over to develop it further. Jean never agreed with this. She felt strongly that Bill had a tremendous contribution to make through his own experience, and that his philosophy had created a feeling of inadequacy that was totally unjustified. Jean knew that Bill's sense of inadequacy was not related to his ability – which was immeasurable – but to his temperament. For, in contrast to his great gifts as a composer, he loved a life of routine and comfort and hated this to be disturbed in any way. Everything had to be run to a strict timetable and he would become angry and frustrated if anything disrupted this. So, even if his compositions *had* been successful, he would have found it almost impossible to lead the unpredictable life that would have resulted. Both Julian and Andrew need to be ready for any eventuality in their profession, but Jean always maintained that Bill would have found this impossible.

Much of this yearning for security stemmed from being brought up in a working-class family where 'ambition' meant 'bettering' oneself. Jean remembered Bill's mother as an 'intelligent but highly-strung woman' who had never quite recovered from the family's early, poverty-stricken days. Originally, Jean thought that she did not approve of her because she always seemed appalled by the thought of her son getting married. In retrospect, Jean realised that her fears stemmed from her deep understanding of her son's personality. She had felt that he would never be able to accept the responsibilities of marriage. After many years of experience Jean came to believe that Bill's mother had been right.

Another side to Bill was unbelievably naïve. Jean would tell of an instance during the war when they were walking down Tottenham Court Road and approached Foyle's Bookshop. Suddenly, Bill stopped to look at a poster outside that read: 'Bring your old Penguins here.' He stared at this for some time looking extremely puzzled, then said to Jean: 'Why should people *keep* penguins in London and, if they do, surely they should look after them properly when they're old?'

John Lill maintains that Bill was one of the six or seven truly great musical minds he has encountered in a career that has included working with Sir John Barbirolli, Sir Adrian Boult, André Previn and many others. Andrew thinks that his father would have liked to have written film scores. He says: 'He certainly could have been a Muir Mathieson, but I don't think he had it in his personality to make the leap. He had a hugely academic cast of mind, which I don't. He could take down an entire orchestral score if somebody played it. And his knowledge of the art of fugue was second to none.'[11] He also maintains that his father's music is entirely about latent sexuality: '*Aurora* is just about the most heightened piece of music I've ever listened to.'

Julian remembers an instance when the late Christopher Palmer came to visit them. Palmer was renowned for his excellent arrangements of music by Walton, Arnold and other British composers and he specialised in film scores. 'Christopher was a very clever musician and he came with me to a performance of *Aurora* given by the London College students at Central Hall, Westminster. This would have been in the mid-seventies when we never discussed my father's music. The students played it very badly, but Christopher seemed absolutely bowled over by the music. He thought it was superb. We went back home afterwards and naturally Christopher began asking my father questions – the sort of questions I would have loved to ask but never dared. He asked him what had made him write the piece, to which my father didn't respond. He then suggested that perhaps the climax would have benefited from the addition of a cymbal clash. After a long silence my father replied: "You think so, do you?" This time the silence was deafening! My father used to enjoy asking the question: "Why write six pages of music if six bars will do as well?' He was just as economical with his words – as Christopher found out! Soon after he died I remember David Lumsden, the Principal of the Royal Academy of Music, telling me how much he was missed at the regular 'heads of college' meetings they held. Apparently there would be lots of waffle about some problem or another and then my father would chip in with one sentence which went straight to the point and stopped all the time-wasting!"

Perhaps the most convincing testimony of Bill Lloyd Webber's teaching skill comes from Malcolm Arnold, who was a student in Gordon Jacob's composition class at the Royal College. Once when Jacob was absent through illness Bill took over his class for two weeks. Many years later Arnold told Julian that he had learned more in those two weeks from Bill than he had during his entire time with Jacob. Yet, this was the only occasion when Bill took a composition class as he always maintained that you couldn't *teach* composition because people could either compose or they couldn't. He preferred to teach the fundamentals – harmony and counterpoint.

To the outside world it seemed that the bohemian 'menagerie' at Harrington Court was carefree and happy, but – with the prevailing undercurrents – this was far from the truth. It was not until the late 1990s that Julian revealed the negative side of growing up in such a dysfunctional household. He remembered 'endless screaming and shouting' and his father, especially, being 'prone to extreme bouts of violent temper. He nearly killed me once. I was about eight. He had a pedigree pet mouse (only my father could keep a mouse surrounded by cats!). Surprise, surprise, it escaped and of course my cat, Perseus, got it. My father started really beating Perseus but I managed to drag him away. Then he tried to strangle me to death.' Apparently Molly and Jean intervened but nobody appeared to consider the attack at all unusual. Julian recognises that both he and Andrew get their drive from their mother, who would never give up on any project she happened to support. But perhaps their drive to succeed was fuelled by the spectre of a disappointed father always lurking in their background ready to haunt them.

Well after his father had begun to drink heavily, Andrew was not only being successful, but also making money, a reward forever to be denied to Bill. Julian remembers: 'My father was proud rather than jealous of Andrew, but the fact that Andrew was also a composer, although in a different field, only highlighted his own failure. But he was always very supportive of Andrew and he had his own quiet way of keeping both our standards up to scratch.' One famous story, reprinted many times, claims that Bill once said to Andrew: 'If you ever write a tune as good as *Some Enchanted Evening* I'll call you'. He never did. But then, Bill had died before Andrew wrote *Phantom of the Opera* ...

Julian admits that when Andrew was earning millions, his father found it very difficult to go to Sydmonton, Andrew's, country home near Watership Down in Berkshire – a mansion set in thousands of acres. It made him 'too aware of Andrew's success'.

Despite the traumas at Harrington Court, Julian was busy preparing for the London première of Sir Arthur Bliss's Cello Concerto at the Queen Elizabeth Hall. It was on 29 September 1972 and would be Julian's professional début at the South Bank. The *Daily Telegraph* found many good things to say about the concerto itself and praised Julian's 'confident and stylish interpretation.'[12]

The success of that London performance resulted in more engagements for the same work. Prior to a performance with the Bournemouth Symphony Orchestra, Bliss was interviewed by the local radio station, Solent. 'For a good many years, the great Russian cellist Rostropovich has been badgering me for a work, as he's badgered most of the living composers, and I had other things to do, but finally I got down to it, and I wrote it – the first performance was at the Aldeburgh Festival, with, of course, Rostropovich playing and Benjamin Britten conducting, and I doubt whether I shall ever get a first performance with two such distinguished artists, but the young man Julian Lloyd Webber, who's playing it tonight is, to my mind, an astonishing artist of promise. He's played this concerto, it must be five times, and broadcast it as well, so he's perfectly confident about it.'

He was then asked about the characteristics of the cello which need to be taken into account when writing for it. Bliss then explained that, while the violin can stand out, the cello is easily covered by the orchestra: 'I think you'll hear every note that Julian plays – he's got a very strong tone, and he's quite a master of all the virtuoso passages for the cello; he is one of the great young artists of his generation.'

But Julian's introduction into the professional concert world had its difficulties: 'Shortly after the performance of the Bliss, I had a "live" broadcast coming up of the Delius concerto'. Even taking into consideration his delvings into obscure performances on foreign radio stations, this appeared to be the concerto's first live performance in years. 'After practising the intricate solo part for weeks, I developed a poisoned finger the night before the first rehearsal. The more I played, the more the finger throbbed and the broadcast on the following day seemed impossible. To make matters worse, I had attempted to save money by booking into a dismal hotel at the rear of Victoria Station, which turned out to be the coldest, shabbiest most broken-down in the city – fortunately long since pulled down.' Even if he had been able to practise, there was insufficient space in his room to draw the bow across the strings, added to which he never seemed to have enough 10ps for the meter which brought the electric fire to life. But, as usual, next day the show went on.

In addition to professional concert-giving, Julian had taken up his scholarship to study with Pierre Fournier in Geneva. This took the form of intermittent weeks when he would travel to Geneva, stay in a hotel and have a lesson with Fournier every other day. It proved a rewarding experience since Fournier was, like Douglas Cameron, the kind of teacher to whom Julian could respond. 'He was a very charming and unassuming man who did not impose his style on a pupil, but encouraged you to develop your own individuality. For instance, I had often been told that my way of holding the bow was incorrect. I've always held it with a straight thumb instead of the bent position as recommended in text-books. I asked Fournier if I was holding it incorrectly and he said: "Just hold it in the way it feels most comfortable." After all the remarks made by Joan Dickson and others, this was music to my ears.'

With Fournier, Julian studied the Lalo Concerto – he had always admired Fournier's interpretation of it – Tchaikovsky's *Rococo Variations*, the Shostakovich No. 1 Concerto and Beethoven's G minor Sonata. 'Fournier was always thought of as a musician rather than a technician but I was amazed when I asked him to demonstrate how he managed the fiendishly difficult passage towards the end of the Shostakovich Concerto No. 1 where the cello is almost covered by the orchestra. Most players fake the horrendous passage-work, but he proceeded to play it faultlessly.' Another recollection illustrates Fournier's modesty: 'One day I arrived at his apartment for a lesson and he was practising the Prokofiev

Symphony Concerto which had been written for Rostropovich. He'd never played it before and was wondering whether to include it in his repertoire; so he asked me, a twenty-year-old pupil, whether I thought he should play it as it was so closely associated with Rostropovich.'

When Julian returned from Geneva his first taste of independence encouraged him to find a place of his own. In the early seventies, a sudden influx of Arabs into genteel South Kensington (which had acquired the temporary nickname 'Saudi Kensington') resulted in Harrington Court coming under Arab ownership. It had been due for renovation for some time and the new landlords decided that this would be the ideal opportunity to turn the already crumbling block into luxury flats. Jean – always the canny negotiator – had managed to persuade her new landlord to provide them with two smaller flats in a nearby block: the first for herself and Bill, the second for Julian. So Julian was near enough to his parents to be in contact, but far enough away to lead his own life. At last he could practise without interruption and Julian began the itinerant life of a soloist. Had he chosen to play the flute, life would have been very different, as he was soon to discover the many hazards of travelling with his cello.

An early taste of the problem was to come when Julian drove his little Mini to Cambridge to play in a 'musical evening' with the television celebrity Richard Baker as master of ceremonies. After the concert, Julian was presented with a brace of pheasants, which he placed on the back seat of his Mini alongside his cello. On the journey home, he was stopped by the police.

'Are you aware, sir, that your left-side rear light is failing to function, which is an offence under regulation...'

Julian assured him that it must have just gone as he knew it was working when he set out. The policeman was not satisfied and began to peer over Julian's shoulder: 'And what, sir, are you carrying in the back?' Julian replied: 'Two pheasants and a cello.' The policeman was not amused: 'May I remind you that it is also an offence to obstruct a policeman in the course of his duty. I will ask you once again. What are you carrying in the back?' Whereupon Julian removed himself from the driving seat to let the crestfallen policeman discover the malodorous game – and his cello – for himself.

Transporting his cello has caused Julian more than one brush with the law over the years but, sometimes, travelling with the instrument has its blessings. One lunchtime, in March 1973, Julian's manager at Ibbs & Tillett telephoned to tell him that Paul Tortelier had been taken ill and was scheduled to play the Haydn D major Concerto in Nottingham that night. Would Julian take his place? Apparently there was a train leaving at 1.50p.m., so Julian stuffed the music and his penguin suit into a bag and tore off in a taxi to St Pancras station. In those days, the first-class carriages used to be made up of single compartments so, as Julian had not played the concerto for at least a year, he decided he could turn one of these into a practice studio during the journey. Unfortunately, his scheme was jeopardised when he realised he had dashed out of the flat with hardly any money and, after paying the taxi, could only just about rustle up a second-class fare. He decided to take the risk and, removing the cello from its case, set about practising the Haydn with a vengeance. Half-way between Luton and the end of the first movement he heard the ticket inspector in the compartment behind. Julian remembers: 'Now what was I to do? Hide in the loo – leaving the cello behind on the seat? Not for the first time I wished I had chosen to play the piccolo and could stuff the wretched thing out of sight. Somehow I was going to have to try to explain. As the inspector advanced I attacked the Haydn with renewed vigour, trying to look for all the world as if it was a perfectly natural thing to be doing on a train to Nottingham. For a moment he hesitated by the door. Glancing up I saw him gazing incredulously at the occupant of his compartment and prepared for the worst. But instead of coming in he shot off down the corridor, obviously convinced an escaped lunatic was aboard his train. Meanwhile, I had discovered interesting new methods both of fare-dodging and of making sure of a compartment to yourself and I returned happily to my Haydn.'

March 1973 was memorable for quite another reason. It was to be the month of Julian's first recording. In 1972, shortly after his performance of the Bliss Concerto, he was approached by a small educational label called Discourses. They asked if he would be interested in making a record as part of their 'Voice of the Instrument' series, which was to be 'entertaining as well as educational'. With great excitement Julian set about planning the repertoire. He chose short pieces by Bach, Beethoven, Popper, Fauré and Saint-Saëns and he decided he would also include the Delius Sonata, a work very seldom played at the time. So, one Thursday, at the Church of St. George the Martyr in Holborn, Julian, with pianist Clifford Benson, made his first recording. Perhaps it was the inclusion of the Delius that merited a review in *Gramophone* magazine. The writer recollects that, as a sixteen-year-old, he had heard the first-ever recording by Beatrice Harrison and Harold Craxton, which provided him with one of his major musical experiences. He goes on to say that there have been three other versions since then, but this is the one he prefers and one that is worthy of a place beside the original recording. There was more: 'Two fine young players on the threshold of undoubtedly distinguished careers could hardly have offered a better *carte de visite* as proof of their musical sensitivity. And the recording has the right kind of resonance to enhance the superlative cello and piano tone they produce.'[13] Thirteen years later, Discourses offered the tapes to CBS and Julian's day's work suddenly reached a much larger audience.

Another 'lucky break' came exactly a year later when his agent phoned to ask if he knew Richard Strauss's *Don Quixote*. He certainly knew it by repute as one of the longest, most complex pieces for cello and orchestra, but he had never even seen the music, let alone played it. He realised that an engagement was in the offing, so he lied: 'Why, yes of *course*, I know it well. Why do you ask?' He soon learned that the soloist with the Royal Liverpool Philharmonic Orchestra had fallen ill and they needed to find a replacement immediately. Then came the news that Sir Charles Groves was conducting and would want to hear him play it before he could be engaged, so how soon could this be arranged? By now, Julian was beginning to panic and wondered whether he should own up to his deceit. He resisted the temptation and, trying to sound as casual as possible, asked: 'When's the concert?' They told him there were four – Liverpool, Wolverhampton, Edinburgh and Glasgow – and the first was in ten days' time, but Sir Charles wanted to hear him as soon as possible. 'When can you take it to him?'

Julian asked them to hold on whilst he checked his diary. Thumbing through the pages, his heart sank. He had four concerts between the present time and the first one in Liverpool and hardly any time to learn the piece. He knew that if he refused they might never ask him again so he took what seemed like the biggest gamble of his life. He said: 'Just give me three days to brush it up and then I'll play it to Sir Charles.' Suddenly he realised he did not even have the music so he rang the main music shops in London to see if they had a copy. None of them had. With mounting desperation he rang Douglas Cameron, feeling sure *he* would have one, and briefly explained the problem. Douggie was not encouraging – 'You'll never manage *Don Quixote* in that time' – but said that Julian would be welcome to borrow his copy. That night, unable to sleep, he lay in bed haunted by Cameron's words, wondering if he'd made a terrible mistake: 'Finally, drifting off, I woke in a cold sweat with a vision of being on a platform in front of thousands of people with no idea of what I was supposed to be playing – the musician's worst nightmare.'

The following days and most of the nights, Julian spent every available moment on the Strauss. When he was not practising it he was listening to it and, by the time Sir Charles opened the door of his flat, it was 'Don Quixote who walked in, not Julian Lloyd Webber'. To Julian's relief, Sir Charles confirmed the engagements. Julian continued to practise furiously and the tour went better than expected (Julian had even managed to play the piece from memory). When it was over, Sir Charles said he was so pleased that he had decided to include *Don Quixote* at the orchestra's Royal Festival Hall concert in three months' time. When the reviews acknowledged this 'shining new talent' Julian wondered what they would have thought if they had known how drastically he had lied to get the engagement in the first place. Yet, his gamble had paid off and the future was beginning to look very bright indeed.

Chapter 5

Variations

Julian's personal life had taken on a new dimension. For over five years, from their first date at the Tortelier concert, Julian and Celia had been going out together. Although they were young, marriage seemed inevitable, and on 29 June 1974 (the day after Julian's Festival Hall performance of *Don Quixote*) they were married at St Mary's Church, Walton-on-Thames, with Andrew as best man. As a couple they were admirably suited. Celia was placid in temperament with a good sense of humour. She also possessed a gift for seeing both sides of any argument. This contrasted with Julian's more volatile approach and his tendency to get ruffled if things did not work out. In retrospect, Celia maintains that the problems both brothers have experienced with their marriages could well stem from the fact that as children 'they were never disciplined and had a willing slave in their beloved "Gran" who would probably have picked up their socks if asked'. Nonetheless, Julian and Celia's marriage worked extremely well for many years. Even now, Julian blames himself for the final break-up. He stresses that Celia was always supportive of everything he undertook and remains extremely grateful today for all her help and understanding.

Celia also recalls that Julian would often ask her to listen while he played a piece through before a big concert because he valued her opinion. But curiously enough he 'banned' her from being in the audience during the actual concerts. 'I could take him to the hall and attend any social function involved but he always insisted I should remain backstage. Occasionally he would ask me what it was like and I would say, "How can I tell you? I only heard through the keyhole. Why don't you let me hear properly?" But he would only grunt and say, "Oh no, I don't want you in the hall."'

However, Celia does remember one occasion when she was not only allowed into the hall but was asked to join Julian on the platform. A festival at which Julian played had had the bright idea of running a competition to find a new piece for solo cello. All the entries were to be sent to Julian who would choose a winner and play the piece at a festival concert. After wading through reams and reams of manuscript, some of which had trendy signs and symbols 'which Julian thought might be good for wallpaper', he finally found a piece he liked. The trouble was that in one passage the cellist was instructed to dash all over the fingerboard at breakneck speed while apparently plucking his open C string at the same time. Having failed to perfect this feat, Hendrix-style, with his teeth, he decided that only two alternatives remained. Either a second cellist would have to be brought in at great expense, or someone would have to wait patiently behind him to pluck when required. He settled on the latter solution and Celia was brought in to make her concert début (only later did they realise she was not a member of the Musicians' Union). Julian recalled: 'If the cello writing in this piece was not entirely practical, Celia's sudden appearance on stage certainly helped to enliven the rarified atmosphere that often prevails at concerts of modern music.'

Another concert of 'contemporary works' at St John's Smith Square confirmed Julian's reservations about 'ghettoising' modern music: 'The atmosphere reached such heights of oppression that even my cello had a seizure and promptly broke one of its strings. I changed it as soon as possible and returned to the platform hoping the accident might have helped to relieve the gloom. But it felt more like a morgue than ever and, in a desperate, misguided attempt to inject some humour into the situation, I cheerfully remarked: "It's always useful to have a spare G string with you." There followed an awful silence and I quickly sat down to resume my piece, feeling thoroughly disgraced.'

Besides championing neglected British composers, Julian sometimes found himself acting as a musical ambassador for the same cause. In 1985 he was invited to give the first ever broadcast of the Elgar concerto in Luxembourg and, afterwards, the orchestra threw a party for all the local musical dignitaries. During the proceedings Julian was approached by a gushing middle-aged lady: 'You are from England, is that right? Now please tell me where is this Elgar from?'

Back home, it was once again a work of Delius that prompted good reviews following Julian's recital on the South Bank in June 1976 with the pianist Yitkin Seow. It was the *Romance* (1896) that was receiving its first British performance after its première at the Helsinki Festival just two days prior to the London concert. *The Times* critic wrote: 'In Mr Lloyd Webber, for the first time since Jacqueline du Pré took the Concerto and Sonata into her repertory, Delius has an eloquent exponent able to draw out the long-spanned sequential writing and make emotional rhetoric out of a style which can easily sound merely prolix.'[14]

By the mid-seventies, Julian was being recognised as a cellist of some stature and his reviews were constantly faovourable. Nonetheless, he was not content to achieve success purely by playing the most popular concertos. He wanted to explore less familiar music as well and was particularly interested in British composers who had been neglected. In the spring of 1976 he had made a CD for the

Decca label L'Oiseau Lyre, with the pianist and composer John McCabe, of four world première recordings of British music. McCabe remembers that he suddenly had a phone call 'out of the blue' from Julian – whom he had never met – asking him of he would consider participating and would he like to include some of his own works? Besides McCabe's Partita for Solo Cello there was music by Peter Racine Fricker, Lennox Berkeley and Martin Dalby.

That discerning critic William Mann, writing in *Gramophone*, was unstinting in his praise: 'Many readers will know what a brilliant and musically penetrating cellist Julian Lloyd Webber is; although young, he has won the highest plaudits. This record confirms them; music may be thankful that he has a special concern about the work of living composers. In case you feel that these are not exciting composers for a brilliant young cellist to advocate, I should say that the Fricker is a powerful work...and a real duo for both performers.' Of the Berkeley, he writes: 'Julian Lloyd Webber's telling articulation and sense of tone colour are deployed exceptionally; he renders to Berkeley one hundred per cent of what Berkeley imagined when the piece was written and the recording gives both partners air and vibrancy in the acoustic...'[15]

In stark contrast, Julian had accepted an invitation to tour Bulgaria. It was sheer chaos and things began to go wrong the moment he arrived at Sofia airport. Here he encountered a customs official with a metal detector who insisted on running his device up and down the strings of the cello whereupon they shrieked with disapproval. Having survived this onslaught Julian tried to hail a taxi. When five empty cabs sped off as soon as he raised his hand, he thought it must be something to do with his long hair and generally Western appearance until his interpreter explained that, being on a state salary, taxi drivers do not need the trade and cannot be bothered with bulky objects like a cello.

Finally a cab was persuaded to take him to the city. He arrived at his hotel to face a check-in procedure 'which was obviously designed to make you believe that you were really staying at the Kremlin'. Finally, he was allowed into his hotel room where three problems were immediately apparent: the room was bugged, the loo did not function and, worst of all, there were no curtains.

He solved the first problem by tuning his transistor radio into Radio Moscow and placing it against the microphone. The loo remained untreatable along with the sewage, but the absence of curtains posed an insuperable problem. Repeated calls to the front desk failed to get any curtains installed so Julian decided to make a desperate attempt to block out the light by pinning up his clothes. As the window stretched from a high ceiling down to the floor this was a difficult task. By the time he had finished, his entire wardrobe was on display to the citizens of Sofia. The view from outside would have been incredible. Julian recalls: 'My tailcoat hung upside down like a demented vampire and various bits of underwear were employed blocking up odd little chinks of light. Trouble was inevitable, but I adamantly refused to remove anything until a suitable substitute had been provided. Surprisingly, the ruse worked, and in no time at all a porter arrived clutching a pair of curtains.'

Musically, the tour was very different. Julian was teamed with the excellent Bulgarian pianist, György Popov, and despite the fact that he spoke not a word of English, their partnership playing sonatas by Vivaldi, Brahms and Britten worked well. But, even though the concerts themselves were highly successful, with fine pianos and a beautiful new hall in Plovdiv – Bulgaria's second largest city – everything was extremely disorganised and they were constantly given wrong travel and rehearsal times. At their final concert in the resort town of Borgas, inefficiency reached a new peak. They had arrived, as usual, in plenty of time for their 7.30p.m. start and decided to go for a little stroll beside the Black Sea. Spotting a poster advertising the concert they wandered over to inspect it. The interpreter let out a shriek as he caught sight of the advertised time. It was three o'clock! As it was already ten past they dashed to the hall and went on stage drenched in sweat before they had even started.

The summer of 1976 was memorable for quite another reason. Suddenly Julian encountered what appeared to be an insuperable problem, one which might easily have destroyed everything he had worked for since he was thirteen.

Ever since he first began playing the cello he would occasionally feel a stab of pain – like the jab of a needle through a nerve – deep inside the first finger of his left hand. Sometimes the pain would be so bad that his hand would instinctively leap from the string but, just as quickly the pain would subside, and he would continue normally and think nothing more of it. That summer, everything changed.

One morning he was playing a quiet contemplative piece by his father. Suddenly the pain struck and his finger leapt off the string; but this time as soon as he put it back, the pain seared again. He was now seriously worried because he realised it could easily happen in the middle of a concert. He took himself off to the doctor but the doctor could find nothing wrong. A few days later the pain struck again and he went to see a hand specialist. He, too, was perplexed as he could find no cause but arranged an X-ray that also revealed nothing. The general medical opinion was that the finger was probably overworked and perhaps he should try a course of ultrasonic treatment. When this also proved useless, he consulted a skin specialist, who seemed just as perplexed as the hand specialist. The pains persisted and Julian lived in constant fear of an attack when he was playing a concert. At only twenty-five he began to think that his playing days would be over.

That August, he was due to fulfil one of his most cherished ambitions: he had been invited to play the Elgar Concerto at the Three Choirs Festival – the historic festival where Elgar had conducted so many moving performances of his own works. The concert was to be in the Cathedral at Hereford, in that beautiful setting on the English and Welsh border where the spirit of Elgar is never far away. During the week of the performance the pain had become more and more frequent. Julian was determined to do the concert but began to fear it would be his last.

It was Jean who came to the rescue. A few weeks prior to the festival she had been introduced to Rosemary Brown, who had caused a sensation with her claims that she was receiving music from dead composers. She had also mentioned that she practised spiritual healing, and the doctors' admission that there was nothing more they could do had jogged Jean's memory. Julian decided that *anything* would be worth a try and with the negative thought that nothing could do his finger any more harm, he rang Rosemary Brown. She asked to see him that same evening.

Celia drove him to a little terraced house in South London and they were shown into Rosemary's front room. After a few minutes she took hold of Julian's hand and slowly, very gently, she began to rub the tip of his first finger. A feeling of heat began to grow inside it to such a point that Julian began to worry whether it might trigger off the pain. When she finished they sat in silence for a few moments, and then she said: 'I think you should rub a little warm olive oil into the fingertip every day. That will keep it supple and it won't give you any further trouble.'

Julian did not believe her, but over the next few weeks as each day went by free from pain, his confidence began to grow. Since that remarkable evening the pain has never returned. Julian recalls: 'That summer was a turning point in my life. Up until then I had occasionally doubted whether I really wanted the life of a solo musician, with all its struggles and uncertainties, but, faced with the thought of a life without my constant friend and companion, I knew I would have given everything I had to play the cello again.'

Needless to say, the performance of the Elgar was particularly inspired as it was perhaps a subconscious expression of Julian's gratitude for being able to play freely again. One person, at least, in the audience that night was profoundly moved by his interpretation. Jerrold Northrop Moore, the leading authority on Elgar, remembers: 'From the first time I heard Julian play it seemed to me that the outstanding character of his performance was, and remains, integrity. Integrity can mean so many things. But in this context for me it means the ability and insight to be guided by the music itself (the dynamic markings, but beyond them the fundamental rhythms and moods) and not by the performer's whims and exhalations.'[16]

The following year Julian received praise for his playing of the concerto by that great Elgarian, Sir Adrian Boult. The meeting had been a private arrangement and in an acknowledgement of Julian's letter of thanks, Sir Adrian wrote to him:

22 March 1977

My dear Julian,
Your very kind letter has reached me already – many thanks for it.

I, too enjoyed our morning together, and I hope you will have hundreds of most enjoyable performances. I feel I was so immersed in the interpretation that I didn't say enough about one, your splendid tone, and two, the overall rightness and dignity and humanity of your performance. It impressed me very much indeed.

Another, totally new, undertaking was on the way for Julian – a collaboration with his brother Andrew, which came about through their support for Leyton Orient. Julian had been asking Andrew to write a piece for the cello for some time, not only because of his obvious gift for writing tunes but because Julian felt he would approach the cello in an entirely new way. For a while, Andrew stalled on the idea, mainly because he wanted to write a piece for cello and rock band and was not certain the cello would work with rock instruments. Also he was constantly busy on other projects. In the end, the final decision rested on a bet made between the brothers on the result of a match between Orient and Hull City – the last of the 1976–77 season. Orient needed at least a draw to remain in the Second Division. Andrew was not convinced they could manage it, but the loyal Julian was sure that they would. The bet was that if the 'Os' managed to get the draw – or even win – then Andrew would finally have to write the piece. Orient battled to a nail-biting 1–1 draw and *Variations* was conceived.

For the first time the two brothers would be combining their two very different fields. Bravely, Andrew decided to write a set of variations on Paganini's 24th Caprice. He says: 'When I started working on the piece I wanted to do what was best for the cello, so I asked Julian to demonstrate the strengths of the instrument – which were the best registers and so on.' Andrew soon realised that the cello can easily be overpowered by stronger sounding instruments and, as they were dealing with a rock group, it would need amplification. 'The cello would be the star vehicle and I wanted the spotlight to be on Julian; my aim was to turn him into a rock and roll star.'

Julian has a different view: 'When we started talking about Andrew writing a work for the cello I was fascinated to see what kind of a piece he would come up with. Perhaps surprisingly, it did a lot for my playing as I had to adapt to a completely different style. I had to re-bow and re-think all the phrasing and at first I even wondered if it was harming my technique, but in the end it was quite the opposite.' When asked if he would recommend the exercise to other classical musicians, Julian says: 'Definitely. I would go so far as saying that if a so-called classical musician is incapable of playing music in the lighter field, then there is something lacking in his musical ability. However, anyone who tries to break new ground will be open to criticism.'

Most of the time the two brothers managed to collaborate without too many disagreements, but there were moments when it could be stormy. Julian says: 'Andrew quite rightly criticised the way I was playing – that it wasn't free enough. And I would counter by saying "rubbish!", which of course, I would never have dared to say to any other composer'.

The minor arguments were nothing in comparison to the drama that was still to come and which nearly caused *Variations* to be abandoned. When the work was finished a superb body of musicians was assembled for the recording: drummer Jon Hiseman, Barbara Thompson on flute and saxophone, Rod Argent and Don Airey on keyboards, and Gary Moore and John Mole on lead and bass guitars. Before going into the studio they decided to try the piece out acoustically at the summer festival Andrew held at his home, Sydmonton, near Newbury, every year. *Variations* would be the second part of a morning cello recital – in the first half Julian would play sonatas with his pianist Yitkin Seow. They rehearsed *Variations* like men possessed and, when the big day came, both brothers were thoroughly on edge.

Seow had been playing in Belfast the night before and in order to arrive in time for the 11.30a.m. performance he had to catch the first 'shuttle' flight, which operates on a first-come-first-served basis. If the first flight is full, another automatically follows to take the remaining passengers. Yitkin arrived at the airport to find every seat taken and no sign of any backup. The next flight would not get him to Heathrow in time for the concert. Back in Berkshire, to fill in time, the waiting group played *Variations* twice which, with hindsight, proved a blessing since it gave the record company another chance to hear the highly unusual combination of a cello with a rock band.

Meanwhile, Yitkin Seow was dashing to Sydmonton, having hired a taxi all the way from Heathrow at his own expense. But, by the time he arrived, the quick-tempered Andrew was furious and sent him packing. This promptly sent Julian into a rage and he told Andrew that he wanted nothing more to do with the project and would be leaving immediately. He then tore upstairs to collect his things. Only the intervention of Celia – who managed to persuade Julian he was being far too hasty – saved the day.

Needless to say, when it was released in January 1978, *Variations* was a phenomenal commercial success. Neither Julian nor Andrew had really believed that this was possible. They had always thought that the idea of a cellist playing Paganini variations with a rock band was a total long shot. Julian is convinced that it became a reality mainly because of the faith that Roy Featherstone, the President of MCA Records, showed in the project.

One person who attended the recording sessions was Melvin Bragg, who was so taken by it that he immediately asked if he could not only make a documentary about *Variations* but use the opening as the theme tune for his new television arts programme, *The South Bank Show*. Twenty-three years later both the programme and its theme tune remain in place.

When it came to playing *Variations* 'live' for the first time, Julian became unusually nervous. He feared that the combination – with its dependency on amplification – might not work on stage. In keeping with the family tradition of nurturing strange pets, Julian had two turtles called Boosey and Hawkes. Just before the band went on, Andrew presented Julian with a metal plaque that read: 'Even a turtle doesn't get anywhere unless he sticks his neck out.' Obviously Andrew understood his brother pretty well because it amused Julian so much that he forgot his nerves completely and as soon as he got home he stuck the motto on the turtles' tank.

Julian maintains that *Variations* was an important landmark for the cello. 'It is a brilliant piece and Andrew was on absolutely peak form. His idea of combining the cello with a rock band was an inspiration, but was much easier said than done. We were very fortunate to have such incredible musicians working with us.' When they were younger, Andrew and Julian had been to many Rostropovich concerts together, including most of the series of nine that so influenced Julian's choice of career. 'Andrew loved the Prokofiev *Symphony Concerto* and the Shostakovich No. 1 Concerto and they really inspired him. I think he was very brave to take the 24th Paganini Caprice, which everyone knew and which had already been brilliantly used for variations by Brahms, Liszt, Rachmaninov and many others. It's a piece that works very well live and we performed it quite a few times, but it was always difficult to get that line-up together.'

Variations rose to No. 2 on the British charts and sold 300,000 copies in the UK alone. It was also responsible for another unforgettable moment in Julian's memory. As Leyton Orient had, in a sense, been responsible for the entire project, MCA made a special gold disc for the club, which Julian presented to the chairman on the pitch before a match with Leicester City. He describes this as 'without doubt, one of the proudest moments of my life'.

Julian also recalls that, by one of those strange coincidences, his first inkling of the album's fantastic success came on the very day his life turned full circle and he played the Dvořák Concerto at an Ernest Read Children's Concert at the Royal Festival Hall. His first ever sight of a cello had been all those years ago at one of these concerts and it was a moving moment for him when, after the performance, he was surrounded by hoards of inquisitive youngsters all demanding to know about the cello themselves. On the way home, he decided to drop in to his local Sloane Square branch of W.H. Smith to see whether *Variations* was yet in stock. To his amazement, there it was, proudly sitting at No. 8 on their LP chart – literally the day after its release. He rushed home to telephone Andrew with the news.

In 1981 Julian was invited to play part of *Variations* in the Royal Variety Performance. The show included a lengthy item called '25 Years of British Pop' which featured everybody from Cliff Richard and The Shadows to Adam Ant.

Julian was playing the final variation. His cello needed to be amplified, along with the rest of the group, so a special pick-up and lead were attached to the bridge of the instrument. He was told that all he had to do was to walk on stage and plug the lead into the input socket, which had been cunningly attached to a very regal-looking gold chair. But at the moment Julian was due to go on stage the chair was nowhere to be seen. Just as his name was announced, someone suddenly thrust it into his hand. Julian had no option but to walk on stage with as much dignity as he could muster, clutching the chair in one hand and the cello in the other, while wondering if the Queen assumed that he always carried a gold chair with a specially fitted jack-plug wherever he went.

Itzhak Perlman was also appearing at the Royal Variety Performance that night – as the only two classical artists on the programme they found themselves sharing a dressing-room. Julian remembers how relaxed Perlman seemed to be before going on stage. 'By some extraordinary quirk of backstage chatter the conversation turned to Bobby Vee, and Itzhak's uncalled-for, if spirited burst into voice with "Take Good Care of My Baby" has, disturbingly, proved unforgettable.' At the performance he appeared sublimely at ease. It was only later that he revealed he had a splitting headache, which became so bad that he was forced to miss the traditional handshake with the Queen. 'Perhaps he, too, was suffering from the tension of the occasion, but if so he concealed it as brilliantly as he played.'

The following year saw Julian take part in another programme before royalty. This time it was a charity concert at Snape Maltings before the Queen Mother. Julian chose to play a short virtuoso piece for the cello: *Scherzetto* by Frank Bridge. It would be its first performance. Back in 1972, Julian – always on the look out for rare British music – was in the Parry Room at the Royal College of Music rummaging through a pile of manuscripts by Frank Bridge when he came across this little piece which had never been played. As Bridge had been Benjamin Britten's teacher, and the Snape Maltings was the home of Britten's Aldeburgh Festival, Julian decided to include it there.

By a strange coincidence, Julian was giving the first ever public performance of Bridge's cello masterpiece *Oration* at the Bromsgrove Festival the very next day. This elegiac and disturbing work had been written in 1930 in a mood of personal grief for the horrors of the First World War. Julian has a great admiration for Bridge: 'He was a highly original composer, but this masterly work remains hardly known at all. During the course of his life, he underwent an almost total change of style. In his early days he made arrangements of folk songs like "Sally in our Alley" and "Cherry Ripe", but he gradually developed an advanced musical language clearly destined for unpopularity in the British musical climate of the time. *Oration* is part of that language, which perhaps explains why it had been neglected for so many years.' Julian's playing with the City of Birmingham Symphony Orchestra conducted by Guy Woolfenden, impressed the critics: 'For Bromsgrove to secure a performance of *Oration* was a remarkable coup;

this imposing 28-minute cello concerto is practically unknown, a situation which will be rectified later this year when a recording by Julian Lloyd Webber, the soloist on this occasion, is issued. His commitment to it was evidenced by playing of superb technical accomplishment and magnificent passion.'[17] The *Birmingham Post* was equally enthusiastic and remarked upon Julian's 'sensitive reading'.[18]

Almost three years before the Bromsgrove performance, Julian had recorded *Oration* at Henry Wood Hall, a converted London church with impeccable acoustics. It is an excellent place to record and is, according to Julian, especially kind to the solo cello. This was Julian's first recording with an orchestra and there were a few unexpected problems. The obscurity of the piece meant that neither the orchestra, the London Philharmonic, nor the conductor, Nicholas Braithwaite, nor Julian had ever played it before. Then there was the high cost of recording with a full orchestra, so only one afternoon and evening were set aside to rehearse and record this complex and unfamiliar score. Julian became increasingly worried about the whole thing and, by the day before, was threatening to cancel it. Celia knew that something had to be done so she suggested that a concert in London that evening given by his former teacher Pierre Fournier would be 'just the thing to take his mind off everything.' But Julian could not face the thought of hearing a cello that night and, to Celia's dismay, took himself off to Millwall to see Orient's League Cup match. As Millwall is not renowned for being the most gentle of football grounds, she feared his vociferous support for the Orient might result in him returning home minus a couple of fingers. However, despite 'some diabolical refereeing decisions – as the lads battled to yet another heroic goal-less bore – it proved just the preparation I needed to set about the next day's recording with a vengeance!' When the disc was released, the response from the critics was just as favourable as for the Bromsgrove

Festival performance. *Gramophone* writes: 'Julian Lloyd Webber commits himself with the greatest sympathy,'[19] and the *Penguin Guide* praises his 'passionately committed performance.'[20]

As Julian's career gained momentum, he received many invitations to play abroad, but he soon discovered that the itinerant life has its problems – namely, how to travel with a cello. When a cellist travels by plane and wishes to take his instrument into the cabin, he is required to pay a full extra fare. It can then be strapped safely in the seat beside him. Otherwise he is expected to put it in with all the other baggage where it vanishes after check-in, is stacked on a trolley and shot into the hold – the procedure being repeated in reverse on arrival at the destination. Quite apart from potential damage, for which the airline will accept no responsibility, a valuable instrument could easily be stolen during any of these processes.

Julian discovered almost immediately that, even if the plane is almost empty, the rules still apply. He remembers only too well his first experience of the problem. He was booked on a flight to Dublin and made several phone calls to the airline prior to the journey saying he was travelling with a valuable instrument which he would like to take into the cabin. They reassured him that it would be all right as there were many spare seats. Yet, when he arrived at the check-in no one had any knowledge of his messages and the battle, that was to become all too familiar, began. 'You must pay a full fare,' the airline insisted. Julian pleaded: 'Surely it could go half-fare. It doesn't eat, drink or smoke and it's much quieter than other passengers – at least when it's in its case.' It was useless. Even his request to see it loaded into the hold was refused. 'We must have our rules,' explained the official. 'Once we let *you* bring your cello on, *every* passenger will want to.' Julian mused on the spectacle of a hundred cello concertos being performed in Dublin on the same night, but realised he was beaten. This time, he gave in, but it was a mistake he would never repeat.

When he arrived in Dublin he inspected the cello only to find the heavy ebony fingerboard had been severely damaged and the instrument had only narrowly escaped being broken to pieces. The rest of the afternoon was spent rushing from one repairer to another in order to try to get it restored for the performance. It was obviously impossible and it was only through the kindness of one of the orchestral members who lent him her own cello that the concert was not cancelled.

Chapter 6

By Any Other Name

Out of the many lessons that Julian had to learn in a very short time perhaps the most important one was that a soloist must always give their best on each and every occasion no matter what conditions prevail. In the autumn of 1977, he gave five performances of the Elgar Concerto in quick succession with the Bournemouth Symphony Orchestra. One of these was a Radio 3 studio broadcast the morning after their third concert, which had been at Plymouth before a large and appreciative audience. After the intensity of the performance, a late night and the drive back to Bournemouth, Julian awoke to a particularly dismal South Coast morning. The last thing he felt like was playing the concerto all over again into an anonymous microphone.

Eight months later he opened the *Radio Times* to discover the broadcast was not only going out at peak time in the evening on both Radios 3 and 4, but had also been given star billing, complete with a photo of Julian and extracts from reviews of his previous Elgar performances. Suddenly everyone was telephoning promising to tune in and he felt as if the whole world would be listening. He remembered little of the broadcast but began to panic in case it had been as dismal as the Bournemouth morning. But Julian lad learned his lesson well: Sir Georg Solti was among the listeners and invited Julian to perform the Concerto with him and the London Philharmonic Orchestra at the Royal Festival Hall in November 1979.

This was Julian's first encounter with the baton of Sir Georg and it also happened to be the first time that Solti had conducted the work. A few days before the performance Julian went to Sir Georg's home to prepare for the concert: 'I found it fascinating to work so closely with the great man on a concerto that I had played many times but which was completely fresh for him. I thought it strange that he had never done the concerto before because he was quite an Elgarian, so I was able to observe at close quarters the way he approached a masterpiece, free from any preconceived ideas. For instance, the slow movement was certainly one of the best accompaniments I had had so far. The opening is in two bar phrases with a tenuto at the end of the second bar. The writing is spare and it must be quiet, so if the tenutos are not timed exactly right it can easily fall flat. You need a strong lead from the conductor at the start of each of these little phrases. I had been warned that Solti was very strict and might have too rigid an approach to the Elgar but I soon discovered that this was just another of those reputations that seem to grow around certain musicians – *especially* conductors – which are not just misleading, but inaccurate. Solti's reputation for being a hard-driven conductor was entirely wrong, not least with this concerto. In the opening, he had complete control, but within that, he gave me tremendous freedom.'

However, although the performance was well received by the audience and had some reasonably good reviews, there was one which was quite the reverse. In those days, reviews were always published the following day. This was such a big concert that Julian decided he could not wait for the morning and he and Celia set off to Fleet Street to buy all the papers as soon as they came off the press. When he read the review in the *Guardian* he was in for a shock. Julian thought the concert had gone well, but in Edward Greenfield's opinion the Elgar was 'the disappointment of the evening. Lloyd Webber failed to spark off the necessary sense of spontaneity, although with his natural gravity of expression he consistently commanded attention, whether in his unmannered lyricism or in the way he gave Mendelssohnian lightness to the Scherzo. But there were tensions still to be sorted out.'[21]

Until then, Greenfield had always been enthusiastic about his playing but suddenly – at one of Julian's most important engagements so far – Greenfield seemed to have turned against him. Julian began to ask the question why and came to the conclusion that, if he was going to succeed on the big occasions, he would finally have to acquire a better cello. Until now, he had been playing an instrument, possibly by Grancino, dated 1690, which was adequate for chamber music, but it did not have the carrying power that was needed now that he was regularly performing with large orchestras. Greenfield's review forced him to face the fact that he had to find a better instrument. In retrospect, it turned out to be a blessing in disguise.

So a serious quest for a new cello began. Julian started asking around to see what he could find and, after several months, it was a *viola* player in the Royal Philharmonic Orchestra who came to the rescue. His wife was a cellist who happened to have a spare instrument that she wanted to sell. It was a Joseph Guadagnini dated 1791. Celia remembers when they went to look at it. She heard Julian trying it out and said to herself 'Wow! *That's* better.' Julian also liked it and soon was coaxing more and more response from it. He decided to take it and it was not long before everyone started to remark on the way in which he was now projecting his tone.

On reflection, Julian remembers that he did have enormous problems with the Grancino. His friends would say that his sound was not coming across but he thought it must be his fault. 'I thought perhaps there was something I could do to the cello to help it project more. Maybe I should put on different strings, maybe I should change the bridge. I thought of everything, but it was only after Greenfield's review that I knew I had to change the instrument. One thing I do remember is that I had three offers to record the Elgar before I actually did, but I'd always hesitated because I felt the time was not right. I am so glad I stuck to those decisions.'

Julian had progressed to a full-size Hill cello when he was twelve and thinks it is best to play a full size as soon as possible. He then moved on to a cello by Paul Bailly – who was a pupil of Vuillaume – but reluctantly he had to sell it to buy the Grancino. However, the Guadagnini not only had a greater range of tone than the Grancino but was also much richer. He says: 'There is a saying that one should never blame the instrument and in many ways this is true. Ninety per cent of playing is the player, but there comes a point when you can't get more than a certain amount out of an instrument. And I was beginning to feel that I needed that extra ten per cent. In a place like the Royal Festival Hall, which is hardly favourable to any stringed instrument, unless you have a really powerful cello, it cannot be heard. Audiences today have become so accustomed to recorded sound that they will go to a concert and come away disappointed because there wasn't a microphone right in front of the cello.'

Be it Grancino or Guadagnini, 'projection' is especially important on the cello, because when it comes to being heard there are always problems. Julian says: 'I will never forget the first time I sat down with an orchestra and experienced this incredible volume all around me. You have to able to project an enormous sound to be heard above the brass and the woodwind.' He feels that young players ambitious to be soloists must work very hard on projection, because it is something that always has to be borne in mind in the concert hall.

For Julian, variety is not only the spice of life, but an essential way to keep abreast of it. After he had played at Lord Rosehill's open air theatre at Fair Oak in Sussex in the summer of 1978, the organisers asked him if he would like to come back the following year and première a piece by the composer of his choice. Obviously it was an offer he could not refuse. As a long-time admirer of both John Dankworth and his wife, Cleo Laine, he suggested that they commission Dankworth – on the condition that he would agree to play in the piece as well. The result was a work of nine short movements for cello and saxophone quartet called *Fair Oak Fusions,* named after Lord Rosehill's estate. Julian was particularly interested in the unusual combination of instruments. He had already appreciated Dankworth's saxophone writing in his score for Joseph Losey's film *The Servant.*

But there were problems with the first performance. It seems that two weeks before the first concert not a note of the piece had appeared. To make matters worse, Dankworth and Julian had agreed to do a radio interview around that time. 'Sure enough, the inevitable question was asked – "How was the piece going?" I listened intently to John's reply. "Well, you know," he said, "I like working under pressure and it's sort of coming along nicely in my mind."' With a week to go it remained in John's mind and bits and pieces only started to filter through days before the première. But no sooner had the ink dried on the manuscript than it disappeared again. To protect the musicians from the elements, the concerts were held in what was called a 'specially-constructed super-structure' – in other words, a tent. On the day of the performance, in the middle of the piece, a violent thunder-storm erupted, which proved too much for even the expensive superstructure to bear and a severe leak developed roughly above Julian's music stand. As rain began to splash all over the manuscript, notes were vanishing almost as fast and in some cases faster than he could play them. If some perceptive individual had not photocopied the parts, the performance would have been *Fair Oak Fusions'* last!

*

Julian's enthusiasm and, in particular, his dedication to British music was now beginning to earn him a big reputation. His reviews from this time show that he was being taken seriously by the critics and public alike. At the start of 1980, Julian made his all-important US début recital at the Alice Tully Hall in New York's Lincoln Center. With the pianist Simon Nicholls he played sonatas by Debussy, Rachmaninov and Britten and the beautiful slow movement of the Rachmaninov again as an encore. After having spent the previous two hours in an attempt to scale the heights, he left the platform with a curious feeling that something had been 'going on' during the encore. It had.

'How on *earth* did you keep calm through all that?' exclaimed the first bejewelled lady to clasp his hand. 'It must have been so distracting.'

Julian simply smiled, having no idea what *that* was. Gradually the story unfolded. It seems that during the encore a street gang had broken into the hall, run the length of the gangway and forced their way out the other side – terrorising even the battle-hardened Manhattan audience. 'Fortunately,' says Julian, 'the glories of Rachmaninov's music had somehow cushioned me from this slice of New York street-life taking place only yards from the platform.'

The critic from the *New York Times* had either left before the encore, or simply took such disturbances as part of the day's work. In any case, he wrote: 'Such confidence and technical command of the instrument . . . the cellist's musical sensitivity was never in doubt.'[22]

The return flight from Kennedy airport was also memorable due to the all too familiar problems of transporting his cello. He had made special arrangements with the now sadly defunct Laker Airlines for a free advertisement in the programme on condition that the cello was allowed on to the plane – not on a seat, but in the cupboard where the cabin staff put their coats. Despite a letter from the airline authorising him to take it on, when it was his turn to board the aircraft, he was stopped by a security guard.

Quickly, Julian produced his letter.

'Who's it from?' snapped the officer, shoving the letter aside.

'The airline.'

'That's got nothing to do with *me. I'm security,* and you're not going past here with *that.*'

'But if you read the letter you can see everything's been arranged . . .'

'Either check it in as baggage or stay behind. Next passenger,' he bawled and everyone started pushing past.

By now Julian was thoroughly incensed and started down the ramp himself. Evidently unused to such a blatant disregard of his inflated authority the official made a grab for the cello. Julian jerked free and rushed towards the plane.

'Freeze!' yelled Mr Security in true TV style.

Still walking, Julian glanced over his shoulder and was amazed to see the gentleman waving a gun at him. Rashly calculating that the man wouldn't dare shoot, he continued his increasingly shaky descent towards the – for once – welcome sight of the cabin crew. Julian explained to the captain that he was somewhat concerned about getting a .38 calibre bullet in his back, but he was blissfully reassuring: 'Oh, that's just Mike – you don't want to worry about him, he often gets a bit touchy.'

The month before his New York début, Julian had broadcast the Britten Cello Symphony with the BBC Symphony Orchestra under John Pritchard at Maida Vale Studios. Robert Ponsonby, the director of the BBC Proms, was there and obviously liked what he heard, because shortly afterwards Julian received an invitation to play the rarely heard Delius Cello Concerto with the BBC Symphony Orchestra under Mark Elder at the Royal Albert Hall Proms that summer.

Andrew Clements in the *Financial Times* noted that he 'commendably resisted all temptation to dalliance, keeping the music moving with a clear bright tone.'[23]

If asked to single out one of Delius's works for cello, for Julian: 'It has to be the concerto. This rapturous piece, with its abundance of beautiful melodies and ravishing orchestral textures, is a luscious paradise garden of cello sound.' Nevertheless when he was asked to make his Prom début with the concerto, he was more than a little concerned because the piece was so quiet and contemplative. He knew that many of the audience would be hearing it for the first time and wondered if Delius's 'timeless musings' might be lost in the vast spaces of the Royal Albert Hall. His fears could not have proved more unfounded for he confessed: 'I have rarely known a more rapt and attentive audience. It was a moment to treasure forever.'

The following November, Julian gave an almost definitive recital of British cello music at the Wigmore Hall. On his own, he played Benjamin Britten's Third Suite for Cello. With Eric Parkin, he played John Ireland's Sonata in G minor and Frank Bridge's Elegy and *Scherzetto* and, to crown the evening, Julian was joined in the Delius Sonata, by the eighty-seven-year-old Eric Fenby, who had acted as Delius's 'amanuensis' when the composer was blind and paralysed in the 1920s. Julian had first met Eric Fenby while still at the College. It was an inauspicious beginning. Fenby had come to talk about Delius and it was Julian's father who introduced his son to the visiting legend. Julian was totally in awe of the man who had lived and worked with a composer whose music he loved. He had just seen the Ken Russell film about Delius and told Fenby he thought that the music chosen for the film was a mistake as it was not the composer's best. It was a typical teenage *faux pas* which Fenby took without offence, but Julian later realised that the film had obviously centred around the music that Delius and Fenby had worked on together. Clearly

Above: Bill Lloyd Webber in his thirties.

Left: Jean at the time of her marriage in 1942.

Above: Molly (with Mimi on her shoulder) on the roof of Harrington Court.

Right: Julian (right) and Andrew feeding pigeons in Trafalgar Square.'

The first photograph of Julian on stage, at Central Hall, Westminster, flanked by his grandfather (far left) and his father (far right)

IN AID OF WESTMINSTER INTERNATIONAL CENTRE
(SECTION FOR TREATMENT OF DRUG ADDICTION)

HAYDN
PROKOFIEV
CHOPIN

SONATA IN G MINOR
TOCCATA
BALLADE IN G MINOR

JOHN LILL (Piano)

SAINT SAENS

CELLO CONCERTO No.1 IN A MINOR

JULIAN LLOYD WEBBER ('Cello)

BACH
LLOYD WEBBER
SIBELIUS

TOCCATA & FUGUE IN D MINOR
ARIETTA
FINLANDIA

W.S. LLOYD WEBBER (Organ)

AND   JOSEPH AND THE AMAZING DREAMCOAT
by ANDREW LLOYD WEBBER and TIM RICE
A MODERTORIO
THE MIXED BAG   DAVID BALLANTYNE   DAVID DALTREY
CHOIR AND SCHOOL OF COLET COURT
conducted by ALAN DOGGETT

Admission by PROGRAMME ONLY Minimum Price 2/6
From Westminster Central Hall or
10, Harrington Court, Harrington Road, London, S.W.7.

Above: A family picnic (from left: Julian, Bill, Andrew and John Lill)

Left: …an historic night in April, 1968.

Right: William Lloyd Webber with Perseus.

Below: The poster for Julian's Wigmore Hall debut in December, 1971.

Wigmore Hall
Manager: William Lyne

Tuesday 7th. December at 7.30

New Era International Concerts present

Julian Lloyd Webber
CELLO
Clifford Benson
PIANO

'Young Musicians Series'

Tickets: £1 80 50 30 from Wigmore Hall (01-935 2141) & usual agents

Below: Julian's first wife, Celia Ballantyne.

Twenty-six-year-old Julian at the first performance of *Variations*.

Above: Julian with Lorin Maazel (far left) and Andrew (centre) at the recording of the orchestral version of *Variations*. © Clive Barda Photography

Below: At home with the Rodrigos. © Clive Barda Photography

Right: Julian with Jacqueline du Pré after his concert in aid of the Multiple Sclerosis Society in 1984. © Universal Pictorial Press

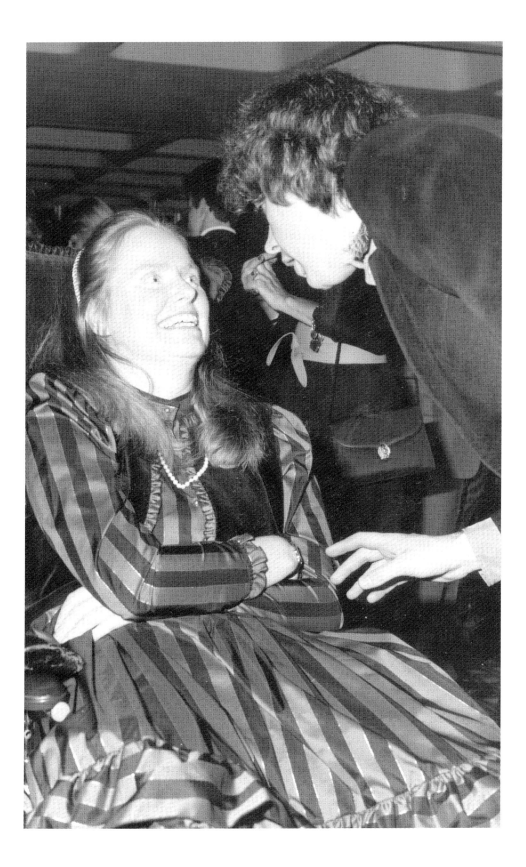

...playing Elgar with Yehudi Menuhin.

...with Stephane Grappelli. © Chris Willis

Above: The true 'O's' supporter with Glenn Close, Andrew, and Antonio Banderas after Andrew's fiftieth birthday concert at the Royal Albert Hall. © Alpha

Below: A spontaneous masterclass to 'Suzuki' pupils outside the Royal Albert Hall.

Below: Recording the Dvořák Concerto in Prague with the Czech Philharmonic Orchestra.

Right: Julian and Zohra on their wedding day. © The Press Association Ltd

Julian with his son David (aged three). © Express Newspapers

this left no bad feeling because their paths were to cross many times and by the time Fenby joined Julian at the Wigmore concert they were already very close. For Julian their association is a treasured memory. 'Working so closely with Fenby was a truly awe-inspiring experience – almost uncannily like communicating with Delius himself some fifty years after his death. Our recording of the Sonata was actually made using Delius's own piano – played, of course, by the very man who had been the composer's "eyes and hands" as Eric used to put it.'

Early the next year Julian had a less happy experience concerning the music of Delius. EMI's *Classics for Pleasure* label had decided they wanted to continue their excellent series of Delius's orchestral music with the Cello Concerto with Julian as soloist. The idea naturally appealed to him as he considered the concerto to be unjustly neglected and thought that the cheap price of this label would give it the chance to reach a far larger public.

Classics for Pleasure apparently had a deal with the Hallé Orchestra and had decided to use them for this recording. Julian was worried on two counts. Back in 1976 he had been engaged to play the Elgar Concerto with the Hallé at the height of his problems with his finger. He had been in considerable pain throughout the concert but it had still been well-received by the audience and many of the orchestral players had come to his room afterwards saying how much they had enjoyed it. However, it was not long before word came back to Julian's agent that the Hallé management had not been too impressed with his playing and over the next few years, whenever his name was mentioned as a possible soloist, nothing materialised.

The other problem was that Julian was very near to signing an exclusive contract with RCA Records who would doubtless refuse to let him record for *Classics for Pleasure*. The

Hallé were on tour in the Far East at the time but their manager Clive Smart telexed the rather strange reply that the Cello Concerto was 'not Hallé repertoire' but that other music by Delius was always of interest. This seemed odd when it was common knowledge that in 1953, Sir John Barbirolli had conducted the Hallé in the Delius Concerto with the orchestra's own principal cellist, Harold Beck, as soloist. None of this was wholly surprising to Julian in view of his previous experience with the orchestra, but he realised that time was running out because of the impending contract with RCA.

The Delius Trust – who have sponsored many Delius recordings – were approached and, after a few months, agreed to cover the costs of recording the concerto. The proposal was immediately relayed to the Hallé and, much to Julian's surprise, they agreed. In addition they 'pencilled in' two live concerts at Buxton and Chester. Suddenly the Concerto was Hallé repertoire. What seemed odd was that the contracts for these two mid-September dates were singularly unforthcoming and had still not appeared by July (contracts are often signed well over a year in advance).

Then the inevitable happened. RCA offered Julian an exclusive contract and refused to let him record for a rival company. The news was conveyed to *Classics for Pleasure*'s managing director, Simon Foster, whose brainchild the project had been. He wrote a friendly and understanding letter to Julian congratulating him on his new contract.

The Hallé took quite a different view. The concert at Buxton was suddenly 'definite' and had been advertised. No mention was made of the one at Chester. What infuriated Julian was that – unknown to him – the Hallé immediately issued a statement saying that he was 'unable to prepare the Concerto in time' for the concert at Buxton, which must have seemed a little strange to anyone who had been at his Huddersfield performance of the work only a few months before.

For a time, the Hallé remained the only professional orchestra in Britain who had not invited Julian back and he confesses to have felt a touch of extra pleasure when his recording of the Delius Concerto finally appeared on RCA with the same excellent conductor, Vernon Handley, but a different orchestra – the Philharmonia. Fortunately Julian is now a frequent guest with the Hallé Orchestra and the incident is long forgotten.

Julian has often argued that concert promoters are not adventurous enough. Often, he had tried to persuade promoters to include the Shostakovich No. 1 instead of yet another Dvořák or Elgar. 'This concerto has not been taken up as much as it should have been. It's a great concerto from every point of view; it is very virtuosic – good for the cello and the orchestra. It is also very exciting and has an immediate appeal to the audience.'

Perhaps Julian's guardian angel overheard, for in April 1981 a sudden opportunity to perform the Shostakovich arose. Julian was in the middle of a rehearsal of the Elgar Concerto in Manchester when he was summoned to the telephone to be asked by his agent whether he would stand in for a Royal Festival Hall performance of the Shostakovich with the Royal Philharmonic Orchestra conducted by Yuri Temiranov, as the Russian cellist Natalia Gutman had fallen ill. 'I had never played the concerto in public before and – what with the Elgar performance – it turned out I would only have one day to practise it. In a moment of madness I agreed. What my agent failed to mention was that it was also being broadcast live!'

When he walked on to the platform on the night he was in a daze as things had happened so quickly. The audience gave him a heart-warming ovation. But, of even greater encouragement, that hard, yet discerning critic, Peter Stadlen wrote in the next day's *Daily Telegraph:* 'His intuitive yet deeply contemplative sympathy with the work rang out in the slow movement.'[24]

But, in retrospect, Julian is convinced that he should have been far more cautious in agreeing to step in for this sort of date at short notice, especially as he had not had time to prepare the work properly. His advice to young musicians is that such an opportunity may seem tempting at the time, but if the performance does not come up to expectations, real damage to a budding career can ensue. The excuse for accepting such engagements is that the agent will not make future offers, if such opportunities are refused too often. It is a Catch 22 situation that can have disastrous results.

The month before his Shostakovich performance, Julian had released the world première recording of Britten's Third Suite for Cello on ASV – a disc that also included John Ireland's Cello Sonata in which Julian was again partnered by John McCabe. It received – without exception – a phenomenally favourable response from the critics. *The Strad* reviewer went straight to the point: 'Although the Britten was written for Rostropovich it is becoming associated more and more with Julian Lloyd Webber...I cannot imagine this performance being improved upon.'[25] It is not difficult to see why these two musicians achieved such a high standard of performance. McCabe, who has worked many times with Julian, finds him very easy to work with. 'He is co-operative in every way and will always listen to other ideas even if in the end there has to be a compromise. He also has a strong view on music and his knowledge is quite remarkable. He is also meticulous in his attention to detail.'

Every review made it clear that they could not wish for a better interpretation of the Britten and, on Ireland's Sonata, the *Gramophone* compared their performance with that of André Navarra and Eric Parkin, saying it was hard to choose between them: 'In Ireland's first movement especially, they bring more urgency to the music, make some of the points more emphatically.' And of the Britten: 'Webber gives the expected virtuoso performance.'[26] The final accolade came from Edward Greenfield in the *Guardian*, who called it 'the prize of the ASV collection. Lloyd Webber splendidly brings out what might almost be thought of as the schizophrenic side of the piece, the play between registers high and low, used not just to imply full orchestral textures but to interweave opposing ideas. With Lloyd Webber the climax of the *Passacaglia* is extraordinarily powerful, and his commitment is just as intense in the two pieces on the reverse – a brief poignant *Elegy* by Frank Bridge and John Ireland's Cello Sonata.'[27]

Earlier that year, and typically wearing quite another hat, Julian teamed up with the legendary jazz violinist Stephane Grappelli on a BBC TV programme called *Rhythm on Two*, broadcast from Malvern. He remembered that he had always thought that the first time he would play in that beautiful part of England it would have to be the Elgar concerto. But it turned out to be 'I Only Have Eyes For You' and the Paganini *Variations* with Grappelli! The new collaboration came about through a BBC producer who already had Grappelli lined up for the programme and thought that the pair would 'spark off' together. Julian says: 'It was a wonderful experience working with Grappelli. He was not only a lovely man but an incredible performer! His agility on the violin was *unbelievable*.' It was well-known that Grappelli disliked rehearsing intensely and Julian confirms this: 'There *was* no rehearsal! We had something like 45 minutes on the day and more or less worked out what we were going to do. There was no problem with 'I Only Have Eyes' because I simply played the tune and Stephane improvised.'

The following November Grappelli invited Julian to join him in a concert at the Royal Festival Hall. The offer came when Julian was right in the middle of a heavy run of dates.

Their performance was to be on a Thursday and, on the previous Sunday, Julian had a Queen Elizabeth Hall recital followed by concerts in Dundee on Monday and Glasgow on Tuesday. They decided that Julian should take the first plane from Glasgow on Wednesday morning in order to spend the rest of the day rehearsing. Apart from the tight schedule there was a problem in that, only days before the concert, Grappelli was suggesting pieces that were just names to Julian. Somehow he had to acquire copies of these mysterious titles while he was in Scotland.

On the Tuesday just before leaving Dundee, Julian had called home from the station phone-box and was told that the BBC's *Nationwide* programme had asked them to pre-record a number next morning and that, naturally, they wanted something which the pair had not previously done on TV. Apparently they had settled on the old Django Reinhardt number *Nuages*. For a seasoned jazzer like Grappelli, who could improvise anything, any time, this kind of situation held no terrors, but Julian did not even know the tune! So in the forlorn hope that they might have a copy of *Nuages* he quickly rang the only music shop in town. Their response was not encouraging. 'New Age, sir? Oh no, we don't stock punk, sir, there's not much call for it in Dundee.'

'It's not punk,' Julian protested, 'it's an old tune for guitar by Django Reinhardt.'

'I can't say I've ever heard of it myself, sir, but I'll go and have a look for you. What would it be under?'

'Guitar,' replied Julian desperately – shoving another 10p into the slot. Ominous creakings could be heard in the distance, which he hoped were the sounds of rarely-disturbed music cabinets being opened and shut. With horror he realised that it was just the shopkeeper walking off.

Two 10ps later she returned. 'No, sir, it's as I thought, sir.' She crowed triumphantly: '*We haven't got it*. We've got one called *Nuages* though, but...'

'I'll be right over.'

Astounded by the find, he dashed to the shop and immediately realised why they had the music – their last delivery had obviously been around 1933 when *Nuages* was a hit. Julian's luck held when he reached the station. There, complete with the old separate compartments, was an unbelievably rare species of train – a dinosaur of the railways built long before Django Reinhardt, let alone *Nuages*, had been born. It was obviously destined for extinction alongside the Scottish wildcat, but for Julian it more than served its purpose and once again saved by the grace of British Rail, by the time they reached Glasgow *Nuages* was well and truly in his blood.

Even though Julian was now being engaged for concerts all over the world, he had a problem with his surname. His brother Andrew had been steadily producing extraordinarily successful musicals in rapid succession and as a result his bank account had steadily grown by the million. Some of the classical musical fraternity regarded Julian's popularity as being a result of his brother's success and therefore not to be taken seriously. In fact, the opposite was true. In his earlier performing days, when he was immature and not quite ready for public exposure, the press caught on to the name, drew attention to his every activity and catapulted him into the public eye. Later when he was more experienced and clearly demonstrated that his was a talent to be reckoned with, the same people continued to say that he was basking in Andrew's limelight. Either way, he could not seem to win. During his first tour of Australia, after a gruelling round of interviews, Julian finally exploded: ' I really do believe that music is more important than the musician. The Lloyd Webber name is definitely a burden and I am concerned about the level of exposure I am getting here because of it. It also means that people here have certain preconceptions about me that are not true.'[28]

The fact that he succeeded with the general public certainly did nothing to placate his detractors. It was a situation that was to haunt Julian for many years until, finally, he would become recognised not only as an artist in his own right but as a respected musician who had achieved a well-deserved international reputation.

Needless to say, the press never failed to pick up on *any* item of news – if a molehill could be made into a mountain they generally managed it. Julian protested that, when he played with Grappelli or made the *Variations* disc with Andrew, he received maximum coverage by the press but only the music critics paid attention to his many first performances of neglected works. As an example, he quotes one bizarre instance when he experienced the unpleasant condition of having a kidney stone. The pain became unbearable and he was rushed to Westminster Hospital as an emergency patient. Even though his doctor had organised the admission and Celia was protesting vociferously, the hospital doctor refused to believe he had a kidney stone. For three hours he was left literally writhing in agony despite all his pleas for a pain killer. Later the hospital admitted that they had thought that 'anyone with a name like Lloyd Webber coming from the Kensington area was probably an addict trying it on to get drugs.' Celia reported the incident to the Patients' Association and within days it was splashed all over the papers with headlines like 'Is Cellist an Addict?'

What might have interested the press a great deal more – had they known about it – was how the condition was finally cured. One evening, after Julian had spent more than a week in agony, unable to eat or drink and with no sign of the stone passing, Celia contacted Rosemary Brown who had worked miracles with his problem finger. This time Julian was even more sceptical because he could not imagine how she could tackle anything as physical as a stone lodged in the kidney. Rosemary arrived that same evening, placed her hand on his back and began to pray. A short while after she assured Julian that the stone was beginning to move and would be gone by the morning. Suddenly the pain grew much more intense as it began to shift. Two hours later, the stone had passed.

Chapter 7

Spanish Acquisition

With his interest in expanding the cello repertoire, Julian had often thought of asking the Spaniard Joaquin Rodrigo (whose *Concierto de Aranjuez* must be the most popular guitar concerto ever written) to write another concerto. But he hesitated because Rodrigo was in his eighties, blind, and might not have even heard of Julian. In early 1980, over dinner with the photographer Clive Barda, the whole subject of new music was discussed. Rodrigo's name was mentioned repeatedly but Julian voiced his doubts as to whether he could really undertake such a large-scale project at his time of life. Finally, Barda convinced him that there was no harm in trying. The next day Julian wrote to the composer's home in Madrid, enclosing his own recording of the Debussy and Rachmaninov sonatas. 'I thought that the writing in the Debussy might interest him. It is so inventive with harmonics and pizzicato – especially in the middle movement.' Having written, Julian put the request to the back of his mind, thinking he would probably never hear back from the octogenarian. But the following week he received a reply from Rodrigo saying that not only did he know Julian's playing but adding, 'Your musicality and brilliant technique have impressed me. Of course I would like to compose for you a work for cello and orchestra.'

Julian was delighted and letters went back and forth for some weeks until it was arranged that he should fly to Madrid in April to meet and play to the Maestro. He stayed with Rodrigo and his wife, Victoria, in their home for only two days but for Julian it was a 'happy and rewarding experience. I played masses of pieces to him and he played many of his own works to me on disc. We talked a great deal, with his wife acting as interpreter. She was obviously the central figure in his life. As he was blind he depended on her completely. She would write down all the music just as Eric Fenby had for Delius.'

Since Rodrigo had already announced, over one convivial lunch, that he would be dedicating the concerto to his new young British friend, Julian began to wonder whether Rodrigo might, this time, consider writing a piece with a British flavour – a sort of *Concierto de Londres* – and directed the question through Victoria. 'An incredulous expression slowly dawned on the Maestro's face: "No! No!" he choked. "Es impossible! Es impossible!" I immediately retreated to the safety of a discussion as to whether the first movement should have a tarantella or a bolero rhythm and drew attention to a bolero rhythm that he had just played to me from his concerto for four guitars and orchestra.'

Rodrigo was a strong, determined character, as Julian was to discover when he dared to suggest that some parts of the new concerto might be too difficult. '*Es facil!*' he snapped – promptly adding a few more demi-semiquavers.

Julian returned home, having been promised the first movement by Christmas, but it did not arrive. Then he heard from Victoria that Joaquin had been ill and began to wonder if he had been over-optimistic to commission a work from an eighty-three-year-old. Finally, in April 1981, the first movement arrived through the post complete with the requested bolero rhythm.

The two final movements followed in quick succession and

Julian realised that any doubts he had harboured were unfounded. He came to the conclusion that Rodrigo was a composer who thought a great deal about a piece in the initial stages, allowing it to incubate before it was written down.

Now that it had arrived, Julian spent most of his spare time between engagements working on the new concerto and in September he made a return visit to Spain. 'The second meeting was of the greatest importance, because by this time I could play enough of the concerto for Joaquin to comment.' His advice was crucial, especially in the Spanish parts where there is a strong rhythmic element. 'I played the rhythms to him in what I thought was the Spanish style, but he just smiled and shook his head. He then demonstrated on the piano exactly how to play them properly. Everything he said was of value. Two of his closest friends were Casals and Cassadó, so he really understood what the instrument can do. Nothing needed to be altered or cut as, no matter how difficult, everything was playable.'

Although new concertos emerge from time to time, very few seem to appeal sufficiently to promoters or players to enter the international repertoire. Julian hoped that the composer of the *Concierto de Aranjuez* might come up with such a work.

The *Concierto como un Divertimento* received its first performance on 15 April 1982 at the Royal Festival Hall with the London Philharmonic Orchestra conducted by Jesus Lopes-Cobos. The reviews ranged from the highest praise to utter rejection. Christopher Grier in the *Evening Standard* called it 'a virtuoso vehicle for the cellist...I fancy this concerto could really stick in the repertory.'[29] Peter Heyworth in the *Observer* was scathing: 'A divertimento is not necessarily to be equated with a medley of jottings that drifts aimlessly from one point to the next. Julian Lloyd Webber applied himself to this dismal little squib with startling intensity.'[30] Bryan Northcott in the *Sunday Telegraph* went even further: 'A repetitious three-movement pleasantry, lacking the neo-baroque *morbidezza* that has made the middle movement of his guitar concerto *Concierto de Aranjuez* so phenomenally popular...To be frank, not even the most agonised face-pullings of its commissioner and soloist, Julian Lloyd Webber, could convince me that a competent *pasticheur* (Lloyd Webber *frère?*) might not have done as well.'[31]

Looking back on the première and the events leading up to it, Julian feels that the entire occasion was over-publicised. The press were constantly writing about it and it was also the subject of a *South Bank Show* documentary. Some critics panned it not only because of the advance expectations but also because they seemed to expect Rodrigo to come up with something that sounded like Stockhausen. 'After all, he *was* eighty-three and you don't expect a composer of that age to suddenly change his style. Personally I think the concerto succeeds on its own terms. I played it all over the world where it was well received everywhere, but eventually I felt that it needed to be taken up by other players if it was ever going to become part of the repertoire. Undoubtedly, the concerto was over-hyped at the time. One of the things I discovered from that experience is that the trouble with being a performer is that you learn your lessons in public. I am much more wary these days.'

Julian recorded the Rodrigo together with Lalo's Concerto in D minor with the same orchestra and conductor. This time the general response from the critics was more favourable. *Gramophone* gave it full marks. After pointing out the many delights of the work itself the reviewer is in no doubt about Julian's interpretation: 'Lloyd Webber is totally attuned to the spirit of the music, fully equal to its technical fireworks, and his playing is imbued with warmth. He is admirably accompanied and well recorded.'[32]

By the time the recording reached the USA the critics seemed to be falling over backwards to show their enthusiasm. John Bauman in *Fanfare* declared, 'this is one of the freshest new works in years. I predict that it will become almost as popular as the *Concierto de Aranjuez* in years to come.' He added, 'The performance is splendid with Webber obviously very much attuned to the music and completely familiarised with it.'[33]

On a sadder note, the Rodrigo concerto is something that Julian will always associate with the death of his father on 29 October 1982. Bill and Jean had travelled to New York for the opening of Andrew's *Cats*. While there, Bill developed prostate trouble and on his return home was admitted to hospital for what was a routine operation. But years of heavy drinking had taken their toll and he also suffered from very high blood pressure. Nevertheless, he came through the operation and – about two weeks later – he telephoned Jean one morning to say he would be ready to be fetched in about an hour; they were going to give him a bath first. Julian and his mother were leaving for the hospital when the phone rang again. Apparently Bill had had a massive blood clot and they were asked to come immediately. By the time they reached the hospital, Bill Lloyd Webber was dead. He was sixty-eight.

The very next day, Julian had a concert at Hemel Hempstead in Hertfordshire where he was to play the Rodrigo, Bridge's *Scherzetto* and an arrangement of the Adagio from Bach's Cantata No. 156. More significantly, he would also be conducting for the first time. He had chosen Elgar's *Serenade for Strings*. Julian had been talking about the concert with Bill in the hospital and his father had been unusually excited about him conducting. (Recently, it had been increasingly difficult to get him to enthuse about anything.) At first Julian thought that he had to cancel but Jean insisted that Bill would have been furious at the idea. She persuaded him to carry on and went with him to the concert. Just before the Elgar *Serenade*, Julian made an announcement saying that he would like it to be in the memory of his father. It was a moving experience for all concerned.

Later the family learned that Bill's entire worldly goods consisted of his music and £1000. The rent of their flat had been paid for by the London College and Bill had cleverly added a proviso that this arrangement should continue for the rest of Jean's life. Julian and Andrew knew that he was not wealthy but it was a shock to find that he had almost nothing to show for a lifetime of hard work.

Bill had virtually given up composing in the early fifties, but twenty-five years later everything changed when Justine Bax – a distant relative of the composer Arnold Bax – became a student at the London College of Music. Born in Ashford in Kent in 1952 Justine had shown early signs of musical talent. She possessed a fine dramatic soprano voice and her greatest ambition was to become an opera singer. However, her family did not have the money for expensive lessons so she trained as a teacher and started working in a primary school. When she was in her early twenties she came to London to have some private coaching with a teacher who suggested that she try for a scholarship to the London College of Music. She was auditioned by Bill, who – obviously impressed by her talent – recommended her for a scholarship.

For the first six months or so she did not see Bill, but he had remembered her voice and one day she was told that Dr Lloyd Webber wanted to see her in his office. She immediately wondered what she had done wrong to warrant a summons to the director. When she arrived, Bill said that he knew she had a strong 'gutsy' voice and asked her if she would be interested in joining his choir at Central Hall, Westminster. She was delighted and went to the next rehearsal. From then onwards she attended the weekly rehearsal and the services on a Sunday and – over scrambled eggs and coffee in a little café near the hall – the friendship blossomed. For Bill it was to be an Indian summer that inspired him to return to composition with feverish activity. One of the pieces he wrote during this period was the *Serenade for Strings*, a passionate outpouring of gorgeous melody laced with intriguing harmonic progressions – truly a little masterpiece that was obviously inspired by his new-found relationship. Justine was not only talented but she had an ebullient, happy, unselfconscious disposition that appealed to Bill.

Their relationship has been the subject of much speculation, and many presume she was his mistress, but this was not so. When they met, Bill was sixty-two and Justine twenty-three. Certainly they were soul mates with a tremendous amount in common and Justine admits that, had they been of a similar age, their relationship might have been very different. As it was she had a great affection for him and tried hard to make him believe in his abilities as a composer. Although he resumed composing during the few years of their relationship, she, too, had to battle with his innate pessimism and paranoiac obsession that he was a failure. Today, she still has no doubt about his talents: 'He was a brilliant man on so many levels, but he didn't accept it himself. He was very self-effacing, never over-confident and he never bragged. And although he was so withdrawn about his own ability, once he was in composition mode he couldn't stop. He was in a burning passion until the piece was finished.'

Bill obviously adored Justine but the extent and true nature of the affection he felt for her is open to question. He would say that real love existed only in dreams and that its reality could never be found on earth. The truth was that Bill found in Justine a confidante with whom he could talk about his family and their aspirations in a way he could never show them face to face.

Justine Bax became well known to the family and, once Jean had decided that she was not a threat to her marriage, the two got along very well. When Justine's scholarship ran out and she could not afford to pay for further tuition, it was Jean who organised a job for her at Wetherby School where she herself taught. Justine is emphatic that Bill never asked her to marry him and, even if he had, she would not have accepted him. She is equally emphatic that Bill would never have left his wife under any circumstances. Justine was a frequent visitor to their home when Bill was alive and after his death she continued to see Jean. Apparently, Bill often said that Justine was a substitute for the daughter he never had. And it is more than possible that Jean, in her heart, felt the same.

Justine also sheds some light on the problems that had existed between Bill and Jean. She confirms that Jean was a woman who took no pride in her appearance, which was something Bill found difficult to accept. He admired beauty and beautiful things and tended – in his old fashioned way – to place a woman on a pedestal. It seems that throughout their marriage, Bill constantly asked Jean to buy herself new clothes and gave her the money to do so. But she continued to buy everything from charity shops and, even when she attended Andrew's first nights, she would arrive in some dowdy bargain outfit when her son would have liked her to appear in something sparkling and fashionable. (Julian maintains that she never went to a hairdresser in her life.) Bill loved to dine out whereas Jean cared nothing about socialising in any form. So it was Justine whom Bill took to the Chelsea Arts Club, where he was a member, and to the Ivy or the Café Royal where the waiters all knew him. Again, Jean had no interest in food as long as it was palatable and served its purpose and it was hardly surprising – when Bill had the chance of a lively companion who was also a kindred spirit – that he spent time (and most of his money) on enjoying his good fortune. Justine admits that for her it was a wonderful opportunity to be spoiled. 'For the first time in my life I was introduced to fine food and fine wines.' She also remembers Bill's obsession with punctuality. 'Everything he did had to be at exactly the same time. He would go through a daily ritual of being home at exactly eleven o'clock each night. Tea had to be at five and dinner at seven. If I was two minutes late, he would be furious.'

Both Bill and Jean seemed incapable of showing any outward or tactile sign of affection. Perhaps it was this inability to express themselves emotionally that caused them to lavish so much attention on their pets?

Jean was totally desolated by Bill's death. Clearly she had feelings of guilt that perhaps she had not done enough to help him. Perhaps she also remembered that she had never heeded any of his suggestions to make herself attractive.

A few months after Bill's death, Jean began to have inexplicable chest pains. She went for some tests, which showed she was suffering from breast cancer and needed an operation. She had always had a fear of cancer, but refused to have an operation as she believed it would not work and thought it would in fact accelerate the disease. Instead she took the anti-cancer drug Tamoxifen, which is known to cause depression. From this time, Jean was severely affected and would go into long periods of absolute silence that could not be broken.

Chapter 8

The 'Barjansky' Strad

Julian's taste in music had always been far-reaching. He had long admired the music of the singer/songwriter Peter Skellern and particularly liked the way he wrote for brass band. So, in 1982, he asked Skellern to write something combining brass and cello. Skellern delivered a piece that started out as *Five Love Songs* for cello, piano, vocals and brass quintet. It was premièred successfully at the Salisbury Festival in 1982 and the reaction from the invited record companies meant that it would certainly have a life after the festival. It was taken by Warner's but they wanted to change it and 'come up with a concept'. Their idea was to form a band and also to bring in a female vocalist. Julian admits he did not like the idea: 'But I wanted to record with Peter so joined what became Oasis. Yes, we were the first Oasis!'

Julian's disappointment increased when it was decided to cut the brass out altogether and substitute a synthesiser sound. 'It had previously been a very interesting idea combining Peter's highly distinctive piano and vocal style, the brass quintet and my cello, but everything got changed. Mary Hopkin was brought in as the female vocalist and we recorded a whole album with the new line-up. But I decided that I'd had enough when they substituted a funky version of Stevie Wonder's 'Superstition' with the old Cole Porter classic 'True

Love'. In 'Superstition' I'd devised a phrase that I played in octaves on the cello. It sounded quite original. As soon as the record company heard it they said it wasn't what they had in mind for the group – they wanted something more "easy listening". But the trouble with being "middle of the road" all the time is that you can end up being hit by a truck!'

Soon after the album's release in 1984, Julian left Oasis. 'I felt the project had been hijacked by the record company. Why do they find something they like and then set about changing it into something completely different?'

Soon after Oasis, Julian took what was arguably one of the most important decisions of his life. The 'Barjansky' Stradivarius cello came up for auction at Sotheby's in London and Julian decided to bid for it. For some time he had known that his Guadagnini instrument was not the final answer and he had been trying out various cellos which were up for sale. But, as any string-player will admit, it is the almost human relationship between player and instrument that is the deciding factor. When Julian tried the 'Barjansky' he knew that it was the instrument for him. He decided to stake everything he had – and more – on bidding for this rare beauty and vowed to move heaven and earth to possess it.

When the auctioneer's hammer finally fell, the price was £175,000 (the final sum would be nearer £200,000 with the auctioneer's commission) and Julian set about trying to find a way to pay for his new acquisition. He sold his Grancino cello and withdrew his life savings but was still well short of the full amount. He asked Andrew for a loan, but Julian recalls: 'He was getting divorced from his first wife and said he couldn't lend me the money because he didn't have it.' Julian was compelled to take out a loan and not for the first time wished his name was Smith! When he approached the building society he was greeted with disbelief. His brother had three shows running at the same time – a record for any composer, living or dead, so nobody seemed to want to lend a Lloyd Webber any money.

Celia had encouraged Julian to bid for the Strad because she knew that such an opportunity would probably never come again. She recalls that when his bank refused to give him a loan they went to Bristol to see the manager. Julian and Celia had a small country home in Northamptonshire and they convinced the bank manager to drive in convoy to the house for the sole purpose of deciding whether – should the need arise – the sale of the property would be enough to cover the value of a loan. Eventually he agreed that it would and at last Julian had found a way to raise the money.

After his struggle to buy the Strad, Julian recalls with amusement what happened the very first time he played it. He was taking part in a TV programme and noticed one of the cameramen looking more and more disconcerted as he gazed through the lens, focusing on the instrument's aged front. Finally, he exclaimed in disgust: 'Cor Blimey! You'd think he'd 'ave bothered to buy a new one for the TV!'

The following August Julian gave the first modern performance – and only the second ever – of Vaughan Williams' *Fantasia on Sussex Folk Tunes* at the Three Choirs Festival in Gloucester. Once again it was Julian's indefatigable curiosity that led to its rediscovery. He had known of its existence through a biography of the composer by Michael Kennedy. Apparently, it was about fifteen minutes long and had been given its première by Casals in March 1930 with the Royal Philharmonic Orchestra under Barbirolli. 'I always thought it strange that it seemed to have totally disappeared. Kennedy wrote warmly about it and knew the composer wanted to revive it. I decided to phone the composer's widow, Ursula, to ask what had happened to it. She told me that most of the composer's manuscripts, including the *Fantasia*, were given to the British Museum. Apparently, Vaughan Williams had not wanted the piece to be withdrawn but had always intended to rework it in some way.' Ursula Vaughan Williams was delighted that Julian was interested and gave him permission to obtain a copy from the British Museum. Similar detective work had already led Julian to Gustav Holst's *Invocation*.

Invocation was written in 1911 and had been given its first performance the same year by May Mukle at the Queen's Hall. A very fine player, she was regarded as a pioneer among women cellists.

Again, *Invocation* was never published, but the composer's daughter, Imogen, released the work in 1981 for Julian, who says: 'Although it is only ten minutes long, within that time it covers a tremendous amount of ground, using the whole range of the cello in a very striking way.'

Along with the Delius Concerto, Julian recorded the Holst and Vaughan Williams pieces with the Philharmonia Orchestra conducted by Vernon Handley. On its release in 1983 the critics again paid tribute to his penchant for British music and his mastery of interpretation. The *Sunday Times* noted that 'Julian Lloyd Webber threads the golden solo line *con amore* through one of Delius's loveliest works. Tinged with the gentle melancholy of the autumnal harmonics that were his alone.'[34] The *Guardian* remarked that its only previous recording had been made by Jacqueline du Pré 'playing with teenage intensity' almost 20 years ago , going on to say 'Now Lloyd Webber and Handley present a more richly idiomatic view with the surprise of the Allegramente last section brought out the more.'[35] *Gramophone* was equally enthusiastic: 'Holst's *Invocation* has the great advantage of impeccable performance and the same splendid quality of recording given to the Delius.'[36] From across the Atlantic, the *New York Times* noted that: 'Julian Lloyd Webber is a young cellist who is making a considerable reputation for himself'. Of the Delius, they wrote: 'It is a bright, leisurely score that abounds in sweeping pastoral writing, and lovely, extended cello lines that allow Mr Webber to display his considerable facility without seeming unduly theatrical.'[37]

In January 1984 Julian gave the American première of the Rodrigo with the Detroit Symphony Orchestra conducted by Hiroshi Wakasugi. It was a triple début in that it was also a first appearance with the orchestra for both conductor and soloist. According to John Guinn writing in the *Detroit Free Press*, Wakasugi's approach was 'sluggish and tentative' but with Julian there were no such problems: 'He played the new concerto with conviction and fervor, and with a technique that seems totally secure. He tore through the fiendishly difficult double stops, rapid scales and bouncing bow passages of the second movement cadenza with consummate skill.'[38]

Back in the UK later that month Julian performed the Dvořák Concerto at the Barbican with the London Symphony Orchestra under Evgeny Svetlanov. Julian was a huge admirer of the Russian and had seen him conduct many times. Naturally, he looked forward to working with him very much, but things turned out rather differently from what he had hoped. To begin with, it was the second time Julian had stepped in for an indisposed Natalia Gutman. Svetlanov had apparently asked for him, which Julian thought strange since they had had no previous contact whatsoever.

The two met for the first time at the initial rehearsal at Henry Wood Hall. Julian had been warned that Svetlanov was ill and that the rehearsal would be short. When the great Russian mounted the podium he was deathly pale and went through the motions of conducting 'like a zombie'. A rehearsal was also scheduled on the day of the concert at the Barbican and Julian assumed that everything would be sorted out then. But at the last moment Svetlanov cancelled, so there would be no further rehearsal at all and they would have to be content with this perfunctory play-through. Julian dug in his heels and said that unless he could go through it in some detail with the conductor personally, he would pull out.

So a compromise was agreed and the orchestra arranged for Julian to visit Svetlanov where he was staying. 'I found myself going into an enormous block of flats owned by the USSR in Grosvenor Square – which happened to be right next to the American Embassy – it was just like walking into a John le Carré novel. Svetlanov was still as white as a sheet and was not at all communicative. We had very little time together but managed to sort a few things out. The concert was not fantastic but nothing really terrible happened. Over the next two days we had two more performances, one at the Fairfield Hall and another back at the Barbican and both went much better. Obviously Svetlanov had recovered, but in Croydon he suddenly decided to rehearse the orchestra for hours in Tchaikovsky's Fifth Symphony – which they knew backwards.'

The following month Julian became one of only a handful of British instrumentalists ever to work with the Berlin Philharmonic Orchestra when, under the American conductor Richard Dufallo, he gave the German première of the Rodrigo. As in Detroit, the critic described the conductor as one who tends to tackle things a little too soberly, but added : 'It says a great deal for the elderly Rodrigo's sparkle that his Cello Concerto held our attention so enjoyably and Julian Lloyd Webber...played with fire and passion. He is a captivating and masterly performer.'[39]

Apart from being one of his most important concerts to date, Julian found the entire experience interesting from another, more unusual, aspect. 'The programme was entirely twentieth century music; beside the Rodrigo they played Stravinsky's Symphony in C. What you had was a "Rolls-Royce" team of players not used to this kind of music. While there was some tremendous individual playing, collectively they were having problems. They are not sight-readers like the London orchestras. But of course I am talking only about the rehearsal. By the performance they had everything sorted out.'

*

By 1984 Julian had signed an exclusive contract with Philips and the first fruit of their collaboration was *Travels with my Cello* – a mixture of popular short pieces. It heralded Julian's first venture into the literary world with the publication of his book of the same title. A well-written and entertaining account of the hazards of travelling with such a large instrument, it was well-received by critics and public alike. It also contains many anecdotes about his student days at the Royal College of Music and his earliest experiences of concert-giving.

Another 'first' to be greeted with enthusiasm was the première of the cello and piano version of Elgar's Romance at the Wigmore Hall. Julian first came across the piece through Jerrold Northrop Moore. Although Elgar originally wrote it for bassoon and orchestra, Moore knew that Elgar had also arranged it for cello and piano but nobody ever seemed to have played it – at least in public.

In July 1985 Julian was to record the Elgar Concerto at last. 'There were three previous times when I could have recorded the Elgar but I had made mistakes in my early days by accepting things before I was ready. I was not going to do that with the Elgar because I love it and I couldn't allow myself to get it wrong.' Julian was quite certain that the conductor he needed was Yehudi Menuhin, who as a sixteen-year-old had worked with Elgar himself when he made that legendary recording of the Violin Concerto under the composer's baton. Yet when he first mentioned the idea to Philips they protested that Menuhin did not have a reputation as a conductor and suggested that a younger British conductor would be more suitable. Julian disagreed and said that if he could not do it with Menuhin he did not want to make the recording.

Philips finally conceded, but there arose another problem when it came to deciding what should go with it. Philips suggested Elgar's *Serenade for Strings* and *Introduction and*

Allegro, which Julian thought appropriate. But it was *he* who had to contact Menuhin to ask if he would like to make the recording. Menuhin said that he would be delighted to record the concerto with Julian and the Royal Philharmonic Orchestra but wanted to do Elgar's *Enigma Variations* instead of the string pieces.

When Julian returned to Philips with Menuhin's suggestion they refused. 'We can't do that. We've just recorded the *Enigma* with André Previn.' So Julian went back again to Menuhin, but he was adamant. It would be the *Enigma* or nothing else. 'I was in an impossible position and decided that the only course was to try to get sponsorship for the *Enigma* part of the disc so that Philips did not have to pay. Of course they agreed to that! And then I set about trying to find a sponsor. Eventually I discovered a small company who had been recommended by the RPO's accountants.'

All seemed set but, two weeks before the recording was due to begin, the deal fell through. Julian was bitterly disappointed – and extremely annoyed. He went back to the company with an ultimatum. 'If you let down one of our greatest musicians (Menuhin) and one of our greatest composers, I will go to every newspaper in the land and tell them what has happened.'

Suddenly, the deal was back on!

When the recording was released in 1986 it was a triumph, not only winning the Brit award for 'Best British Classical Recording', but being chosen as 'the finest ever recorded version' of the work by *BBC Music Magazine*. Julian felt vindicated that he had insisted on Menuhin: 'He was wonderful to work with and very good to me personally. He understood the music inside-out and we made the slow movement in one take – which is one of those things you read about but that rarely happen.'

Julian was to play the Elgar with Menuhin many times in

the future: 'All those live performances with Yehudi were what real music-making is all about because they are totally spontaneous. We never knew what was going to happen from one note to the next. He just let the music speak for itself.'

Beforehand, Julian had felt that Menuhin could have been quite dogmatic: 'After all, he was so much older than me. He could have said "Elgar wanted it this way." But there was none of that – just the freedom of expression that I think Elgar himself had when he was conducting. I also played the Haydn with Yehudi and I found that equally rewarding.'

Julian received perhaps his best ever reviews for the recording. For once the critics seemed in complete agreement as to the performance of both conductor and soloist. Michael Kennedy in the *Daily Telegraph* wrote: 'The Cello Concerto receives an affectionate true-to-the-score and altogether admirable performance from Julian Lloyd Webber.'[40] Robert Matthew-Walker in *Music and Musicians* congratulated Julian on his 'admirable interpretation, making it the best of all modern versions.' He goes on to say that: 'Ably and sympathetically abetted by Menuhin, this performance combines character and fidelity, being sensitive, mercurial and moving by turns – a really integrated performance to which I shall return again and again.'[41]

*

To the outside world, Julia and Celia would seem to have had the perfect marriage. She was equable, tolerant, knew how to deal with artistic temperament and supported him all the way in his career. But being the wife of a concert artist is not easy and when she realised that his Stradivarius was the most important thing in his life she began to feel increasingly frustrated. Problems arose at home and, for the first time in the sixteen years they had known each other, rows became a frequent occurrence. The scene was set for a new problem. One day Julian was shopping in the local supermarket and caught sight of a beautiful girl working there. Whenever he went to get the papers in the morning he wondered what she was doing there because she looked 'like a princess'. Much later he would learn that she was indeed Princess Zohra Mahmoud Ghazi from the Afghan royal family of King Zahir Shah. Zohra had fled from Afghanistan following the 'coup' of 1978. She had been fourteen at the time and had witnessed nineteen members of her family being killed in front of her.

Zohra was the total opposite of Celia: full of eastern promise, she was moody, temperamental and exotic. Julian was totally smitten and, from this moment, his already unsettled domestic life was under even greater threat.

In the autumn of 1985 Julian made his first Australian tour playing all the major cities either in recital with the pianist Peter Pettinger or with the Sydney or Melbourne Symphony Orchestras. At first he had planned to go on his own with Pettinger, but at the last moment he asked Celia to accompany him. She recalls that it was a difficult time as Zohra was now 'firmly on the scene' and they were experiencing all the problems that this entailed. But once they arrived she was overcome with the warmth and friendliness of the Australian people and the beauty of their country. They arrived in Perth and were there for one week. Julian gave interviews solidly for two days while Celia wandered around sightseeing. 'It was a lovely time of the year – their spring just going into summer – and I remember watching one Sunday when masses of people were taking their boats out on the River Swan.'

The tour was extremely well organised by Jon Nicholls, an Englishman who had settled in Australia. He was always in attendance for the interviews and concerts and he took them everywhere. And there was certainly no doubt as to Julian's rapport with his new audience. After the first recital in Perth – in their magnificent newly-built concert hall – Bill Taylor in the Perth *Sunday Times* wrote: 'he is very much at home on the concert platform. He seems to know just how much to talk and how much to play,' and quotes Julian as introducing his final

encore – from brother Andrew's *Variations* – with the words 'I
have to support composers who have difficulty getting
played' which must have brought the house down. But
perhaps Taylor's most significant comment was that 'Julian
Lloyd Webber could well be responsible for a renaissance in
the cello. His touring, recording and commissioning of works
for the instrument are very much appreciated.'[42]

He also gave performances of the Rodrigo and Haydn C
major Concertos in Melbourne and Sydney and there were
glowing reports of this 'exceptionally gifted young virtuoso.'
Roger Covell in the *Sydney Morning Herald* wrote: 'The solo part
is agile, diverse in technique and entertaining. Julian Lloyd
Webber demonstrated unfailingly his readiness to meet its challenges. In fact, although the performance here of the new
Rodrigo concerto appeared to be the principal aim of the
concert, its other main achievement was the introduction of an
exceptionally gifted young virtuoso in Haydn's C major
Concerto.'[43]

Having achieved considerable success with his first book,
Julian now published a second – this time a collection of
sayings and impressions of Casals called *Song of the Birds*.
Every cellist worships at the shrine of the great Catalonian
who stood out so firmly against fascism in his land and was
exiled for many years. Julian is no exception. The collection
covers Casals' entire career and Julian showed that he is not
only a good writer but also a shrewd editor. He wrote a
succinct introduction, finishing with the words:

Here, then, is a portrait of Pablo Casals – in his own words
and the words of others. Hopefully, no side of the argument
has been left out. It's all 'in there'; the love of humanity, the
wisdom, the idealism, the courage, the obstinacy, the
inspiration and above all – shining through the pages like a
rare and precious jewel – the overwhelming, triumphant
and *towering* genius of Pablo Casals.

The book's title is best explained in the words of the master himself:

> I began the custom of concluding my concerts with the melody of an old Catalan carol, the 'Song of the Birds.' It is a tale of the Nativity; how beautiful and tender is that tale, with its reverence for life and for man, the noblest expression of life! In the Catalan carol it is the eagles and the sparrows, the nightingales and the little wrens who sing a welcome to the infant, singing of him as a flower that will delight the earth with its sweet scent.

Julian's essays into neglected British music had now become a hallmark and he seemed always able to find new treasures that had been buried for years. Once he happened to be reading Eric Fenby's book on Delius and discovered a casual mention of him playing through a very early piece called Romance that Delius had rather liked. Julian then rang the librarian of the Delius Trust – Robert Threlfall – and asked if he knew what had happened to it. Threlfall told him that although he had been there for ten years, he had never had an inquiry about the piece. He also told Julian that it was sitting right there on the shelf in front of him. Threlfall happened to be a good pianist and they immediately arranged to try it out. Julian was responsible for it being published by Boosey & Hawkes; initially they printed only 1000 copies but it became so popular that they had to reprint it several times. Much later Julian would make a recording of it with the pianist Bengt Forsberg.

On the same trail but on a larger scale, in the spring of 1986, Julian recorded concertos by Sir Arthur Sullivan and Victor Herbert with the London Symphony Orchestra conducted by Sir Charles Mackerras. The Elgar Romance was also added for good measure. The history of the Sullivan was highly curious. Charles Mackerras had been the last person to conduct it in 1953 with William Pleeth as the soloist. Subsequently the score and orchestral parts were destroyed in a fire but a double bass part and a solo cello part survived. So Mackerras, with help from the Sullivan expert David Mackie, reconstructed the entire concerto and Julian was asked to perform it for the recording.

The concerto was another example of neglect. It had received its first performance in 1866 when the composer was only twenty-four, but was hardly performed again. It is not a great work. It is far too long for its material and has many shortcomings, but was a valiant attempt to add another cello concerto to the repertoire.

The other main work on the disc is Victor Herbert's Second Cello Concerto, a first class composition that deserves a much greater place in the romantic repertoire. The Dublin-born Herbert is remembered today mainly as a composer of light operetta, but he was also a very fine cellist and was the soloist in the first performance of his own concerto with the New York Philharmonic Orchestra in March 1894. Dvořák was in the audience and was so impressed with the work that he was inspired to compose his own wonderful cello concerto. Later, Herbert had a bad accident to his left arm and was forced to abandon cello playing and devote all his energies to composing and conducting.

Following the recording, Julian had a rare opportunity to play the Herbert with the Pittsburgh Symphony Orchestra under Michael Lancaster. (Herbert had been the orchestra's Musical Director for many years.) The concert was part of their summer open-air season and Julian was pleased to be able to play it at least once in a live performance.

Although Julian's professional career was going from strength to strength, his personal life was beset with problems. In the two years since their first meeting he had fallen in love with Zohra and his marriage to Celia was at an end. Celia had realised that nothing could save the situation so she left with all her belongings and went to live with her mother. When she was pestered by the press to give her side of the story all she would say was that she was fed up with playing second fiddle to a cello!

Julian's first tour of Japan in autumn 1986 brought a welcome respite from his domestic life. He played the Elgar Concerto and the 'small' D major by Haydn with the Japan Philharmonic conducted by Jiri Belohlavek. Marcel Grilli, writing in the *Japan Times* praises his 'beautifully shaped and warmly toned account of the Elgar.' He goes on to explain that the Haydn is not the familiar one in the same key, but one based on a cello-piano manuscript version discovered in 1948, from which Julian had made his own performing version for cello and strings. He points out that we do not know whether this music is by Haydn or not but says that 'Lloyd Webber's enthusiastic playing certainly made a favourable case for it.'[44]

Julian recalls the trip as one of the most dramatically different experiences of his career. He had travelled with Zohra for the first time and they were put in a hotel on the outskirts of Tokyo so there was no question of walking into the city to investigate, even when he was not practising. There was very little English spoken anywhere and Julian found it quite difficult to understand whether the Japanese meant yes or no as they always nodded. But he also reflected that he loved working with Belohlavek and it struck him that there were no difficulties in communication when he was playing the very English Elgar Concerto with a Japanese orchestra and a Czech conductor: the language of music brought everyone together in perfect understanding.

Chapter 9

A Midsummer Marriage

Judging from the brief snatches Julian had heard of his father's music since early childhood, Julian already knew that Bill had been – at the very least – a talented composer. After his death he was determined to learn all he could about the mysterious scores and to discover the reasons behind his father's decision to stop composing altogether.

Julian knew that some of the music had been published but had no idea to what extent. Soon his natural gift for painstaking 'detective work' paid dividends and – to his amazement – he found that no less than *sixty* of Bill's compositions had been published, in addition to many pieces that had either been stuffed away in a drawer or lost altogether. By 1987 Julian had printed a catalogue of all William Lloyd Webber's published works and had begun a project to have the best of them recorded. Today there are five CDs of Bill's music available and his music is heard on the radio with increasing frequency. Julian says, 'While I was working on uncovering my father's music it was as important to me as my own playing. I kept finding these beautiful pieces that were totally unknown and I just had to do something about it.'

Andrew had already made a start in 1986 by including Bill's *Aurora* as a 'filler' to an orchestral version of *Variations*, which Julian recorded for Philips with the London Philharmonic Orchestra conducted by Lorin Maazel. Many critics were amazed by its qualities; Edward Greenfield described it as 'music as sensuous as any you will find from a British composer'.[45]

The first recording completely devoted to William Lloyd Webber's music was made in January 1987. Julian played two pieces for cello and piano with John Lill, there were songs (sung by John Graham Hall), solo piano pieces and a viola sonatina (played by Philip Dukes and Sophia Rahman). But the main work on the disc was the *Missa Sanctae Mariae Magdalenae* conducted by Richard Hickox. Like *Aurora*, it created quite a stir on its release. Geoffrey Norris commented in the *Daily Telegraph* on the 'instinctive feel for words and choral colouring...a striking expressive force'.[46] Richard Hickox clearly remembers how exciting the project had been: 'Beforehand, I knew nothing of the music and I was both surprised and impressed by its quality. Julian worked fantastically hard to get all the parts for everything on the CD together and I was full of admiration for his dedication.' Days after the ASV disc was made Julian attended the 1987 Brit Awards. He had won the award for the Best British Classical Recording of 1986 for his Elgar Concerto with Yehudi Menuhin on Philips, which was perhaps ironic given the fact that Philips had not wanted Menuhin to conduct the disc in the first place. Julian had arrived at the awards ceremony straight from the BBC TV Studios where he had played an extract from the Elgar 'live' on *Wogan*.

At this moment of triumph Julian's private life was going through all the attendant traumas of his separation from Celia. Although their relationship was turbulent, Julian and Zohra began to consider planning a future together and when Julian made his second tour of Australia (with Menuhin and the Royal Philharmonic) later in 1987, Zohra came too. But everywhere she went there were problems as, being an

Afghan she did not have a British passport, only an interim travel document. This meant that while every member of the orchestra sailed through immigration without hindrance, Zohra was constantly held up and interrogated. When Julian complained to Menuhin about the endless delays he said, 'Marry her – *then* she will have a proper passport!' It seems Menuhin had taken quite a 'shine' to Zohra and was now insisting that she be included in everything. This presented considerable difficulties when it came to the press conferences since a lot could have been made out of Julian's domestic situation at the time. When Menuhin finally introduced Zohra to his wife, Diana, he said, 'Here she is! You remember I told you about her – the wild one!'

Musically, Julian was enjoying the same deep collaboration with Menuhin that he had experienced before and everywhere the critics were enthusiastic. In Brisbane, John Villaume of the *Courier Mail* was ecstatic: 'The Elgar Cello Concerto received a magnificent performance from Julian Lloyd Webber, with perfect accompaniment by the orchestra. We have had several recent performances of the work but last night's set a standard and became an experience never to be forgotten. Menuhin's long association with Elgar bore rich fruit in this searching exploration of the composer's deepest thoughts. Many subtle turns of phrase, often overlooked by other aspirants, were awarded their true value in Lloyd Webber's hands. For at least one listener, this was the finest concert of the year.'[47]

Back home Julian premièred Malcolm Arnold's *Fantasy for Solo Cello* at the Wigmore Hall that December. He had been a long time admirer of Arnold's work and had virtually coaxed him out of retirement by commissioning the piece. The critics appeared to be happy that after a period of inactivity, the composer had 'bounced back with a work generous and direct, exuberant in the way it draws out all the richest and warmest qualities of the instrument.'[48] Paul Driver in the *Financial Times* described Julian's performance as 'articulate, impassioned, large-toned and persuasive'.[49] A recording of the *Fantasy* together with music by Britten, Walton, Rawsthorne and Ireland was issued on ASV the following month. Robert Matthew-Walker in *Music and Musicians* found it: 'another first-class and highly recommended issue from this source',[50] while Alan Saunders in *Gramophone* considered that 'Webber plays this programme with his usual insight and total commitment'.[51] Julian was equally delighted with the *Fantasy*, describing it as 'very effective, direct, appealing and totally true to Arnold.'

A constant factor in Julian's concert reviews at this time was the critics' acknowledgement of the golden tone that he was now coaxing from his 'Barjansky' Strad. After a recital in May, 1988, at the National Concert Hall in Dublin, Richard Pine, in the *Irish Times* remarked:

> In my experience, Lloyd Webber hitherto produced a relatively small sound, but he now has an instrument of wonderful warmth, vigour and personality which is capable of voicing the heavy demands he puts on it in complex works like the Debussy Sonata. It was a joy to me to witness this beautiful partnership between artist and instrument which, accompanied by the committed pianist, Peter Pettinger, found the way, albeit with difficult music, into the hearts of an unfamiliar audience.' For him, 'the triumph of the evening was in the true partnership between cello and piano of the Rachmaninov Sonata. Here, both players showed a sincerity, an immediacy, an elegance, and, in Lloyd Webber's case, a boyish charm, which raised my enjoyment of this gem of the repertoire to new heights.[52]

In June 1988 Julian made his début as the artistic director of a festival with his *Cellothon 88* (the 8s being cannily transformed into cellos on the poster) at the South Bank. Sponsored by Martini & Rossi it was a weekend event featuring concerts, lectures, masterclasses and films. For several years Julian had had the idea of creating a cello festival built round the many fine but lesser-known works for the instrument. In the programme, he wrote:

> Interest in the cello has never been greater – cello concertos are now a normal and essential part of orchestral concert programmes. Yet only a handful, out of many works for cello and orchestra, are heard with any frequency and it is my belief – a belief shared by many cellists – that there are other fine concertos also worthy of our attention. Three of these can be heard this weekend and many others could equally well have been chosen.
>
> Although the emphasis of *Cellothon* is on youth, its many varied events will surely demonstrate the strength-in-depth of British cello playing. This is no mere flash in the pan but an achievement founded on the rock of teaching excellence.
>
> *Cellothon 88* is a celebration of a unique and wonderful instrument and I thank Martini & Rossi for supporting this festival. In 1964, Mstislav Rostropovich wrote: 'The cello, without losing its power to express lyrical emotions and moods, has become in our times a tribune, an orator, a dramatic hero.' These words have a special resonance this weekend.

During *Cellothon* Julian presented several discoveries, playing Bridge's *Oration* and Holst's *Invocation* at the opening concert. But he gave the other solo opportunities to Robert Cohen (in the CPE Bach A Major Concerto) and Raphael Wallfisch (in the Miashovsky Concerto). The orchestra throughout was the City of London Sinfonia conducted by Richard Hickox. Archive films also provided considerable variety and included a profile of Emanuel Feuermann, Beethoven's 'Ghost' Trio featuring Jacqueline du Pré, and the infamous Bette Davis/Claude Rains movie *Deception* in which Paul Henreid plays a solo cellist. Erich Korngold's score for *Deception* later became his cello concerto and the producers fitted Henreid with a special jacket so that a 'real' cellist could work his fingers and bowing from behind him during the many shots of him playing. In addition, Julian unearthed another rare film of Gregor Piatigorsky giving the first European performance of Walton's Cello Concerto at the Festival Hall, conducted by Malcolm Sargent. *Cellothon* was deemed a big success, but a preview of the festival in *Classical Music* magazine had revived the old myth about Andrew having paid for Julian's cello. Julian was livid and the journal was obliged to print the following apology:

> In the *Cellothon* article carried in the last issue it stated that the Stradivarius cello played by Julian Lloyd Webber had been provided by his brother, Andrew. Julian Lloyd Webber has pointed out that this statement is wholly inaccurate, and furthermore that he has no financial links with Andrew Lloyd Webber, nor have any such links existed at any time. We are happy to publish this correction and to apologise for any embarrassment and distress caused by the article.[53]

Ironically, days after *Cellothon*, Julian travelled to Berlin to play *Variations* with the Berlin Philharmonic, conducted by Lorin Maazel, in an open-air concert before 25,000 people. Andrew's second wife Sarah Brightman was also on the bill. Julian remembers the Berlin Philharmonic having tremendous difficulty with *Variations*' syncopated rhythms and Maazel becoming increasingly impatient during rehearsals but, as in Rodrigo's Concerto a few years before, the orchestra was fine on the night.

The following month saw Julian travel to Prague to make

what must have seemed a fantastic recording: the Dvořák Concerto with the Czech Philharmonic Orchestra under their chief conductor Vaclav Neumann. Yet his personal life was in turmoil. Having irrevocably split up with Celia he had had a major row with Zohra and they were no longer together. Emotionally, perhaps, he was at his lowest ebb but he had to travel to an unknown city to record the 'king' of all cello concertos. Julian turned to his old friend Jill Lawrence and asked her to accompany him on the trip. Julian had met Jill in 1979 at his Bromsgrove Festival performance of Bridge's *Oration*. At the time she was the girlfriend of the festival's director, Harold Taylor, and the pair hit it off immediately. Although there has never been any suggestion of romantic involvement the two remain firm friends to this day. Jill remembers the Prague trip as follows:

'Julian had had a terrible row with Zohra and did not want to be alone on this crucial recording. The whole thing was being filmed by Tony Palmer for a *South Bank Show* documentary and Julian was under enormous pressure. Added to this, he was not well. He caught a cold soon after we arrived and continued to feel ill throughout. The situation with Zohra had left him emotionally drained but it was then that – not for the first time – I marvelled at Julian's professionalism. He never complained, except to me – but that was mostly because he could hear my constant coughing through the night as our rooms were next door to each other and I had caught a cold as well! Neumann was treated with complete respect during the recording and was always addressed as "Maestro". He and Julian worked very well together and he allowed Julian quite a lot of leeway over the interpretation. Despite the way he felt, Julian would not let anything pass without it being one hundred per cent in his estimation. He was determined that nothing was going to be allowed to spoil this recording and, as always, gave it everything. Our evenings were spent talking through notes we had made about the recording during the day, although the enforced break between the "sessions" proved difficult for Julian as he was restless to get on with it – and it was giving him too much time to think about Zohra.'

When Julian looked back over recording the Dvořák he had completely forgotten not feeling well. 'It was the experience of a lifetime…it is perhaps the one thing I have done which I would never have dreamed of being able to accomplish when I was a student. I do remember that I was at my lowest point emotionally. I had gone through all the heartache of my marriage breaking up only to fall out with Zohra. Things had never felt so bad but I could not allow my petty problems to interfere with recording God's beautiful music. It is a strange truth that people's greatest professional achievements can be at the moment of their greatest personal unhappiness.'

In between the sessions Julian did manage to visit some of the sights of Prague with a fellow cellist Heinrich Schiff, who happened to be playing there at the same time. 'We had a wonderful time together. It was a few months before the Communists were thrown out and we both remarked how quiet and peaceful the city was.' (When Julian returned the following year to give a concert he was sad to see all the signs of 'freedom' such as the hoard of tourists and the inevitable McDonalds, and thought, wryly, that things do not always change for the better: 'On the other hand I did not have to live under a regime of constant oppression.')

Back in England there was talk about Julian recording the Walton Concerto. On the strength of the success of Malcolm Arnold's *Fantasy*, Julian thought that a new concerto by Arnold would make an ideal pairing and he approached the composer accordingly. The concerto – commissioned by the Royal Philharmonic Society – duly arrived and was given its world première at the Festival Hall with the Royal Philharmonic Orchestra under Vernon Handley in March

1989. But Julian was bitterly disappointed with the piece and claims that it does not do Arnold justice after all. In fact he later recommended that it should be withdrawn.

Perhaps inevitably, by the spring of 1989 Julian and Zohra had overcome their considerable differences and decided that they were ready to share a future together. They were married on 1 July 1989 and, since the bride was a Muslim, they agreed that there should be two ceremonies on the same day – one Christian and one Muslim. The Muslim ceremony was held at her grandmother's house and conducted entirely in Persian so Julian had no idea what was going on. He was therefore slightly surprised when Zohra's uncle suddenly broke into English with the question: 'How much will you pay?' 'What for?' Julian replied. 'It's a custom – a formality – you have to pay something for Zohra', responded the uncle. Startled, Julian asked, 'How much is she worth? Twenty pounds?' There was much amusement and a chequebook was produced there and then. After a second 'marriage' at the Central Hall Westminster a reception was held at Bill's old London College of Music. The honeymoon was spent in the Lake District and ten days later they moved into the house Julian had bought near Chipping Campden in Gloucestershire. A new chapter in Julian's life began and he was looking forward to a more tranquil future with his beautiful bride.

Julian's concert schedule was now unremitting. Weeks after he and Zohra were married, he travelled to Washington with his pianist John Lenehan to give a recital at the Kennedy Center. Before playing Benjamin Britten's Sonata Julian explained to the audience how, when he was about thirteen, he had heard Rostropovich and that the experience had inspired him to become a cellist, and therefore he would like to dedicate his performance to 'that great man of the cello.' In his review, Joseph McLellan from the *Washington Post* wrote: 'Britten's music is enormously demanding, not only in its sometimes manic tempos and advanced techniques but also in its requirements for intense emotional expression, witty dialogue and sound effects that range from an ominous buzz to eerie, high-pitched glissandi. Lloyd Webber and Lenehan rose impressively to the challenges.'[54] As an encore Julian played the Bridge *Scherzetto*, but it was the second encore that had the audience in the palm of his hand. With a deadpan expression, Julian announced that it was the work of a 'struggling composer who has a hard time getting his music played and making ends meet.' It was, of course, part of Andrew's *Variations*.

Lenehan – a student at the Royal College – had first met Julian in the early eighties and was delighted when Julian invited him to take part in a recital barely a year after he had finished his studies. 'Julian was already very well known and I owe a great deal to him for giving me the opportunity to take part in concerts which would ordinarily never have come my way at that early stage. Since the mid-eighties we have given many recitals in the main cities of Europe. Although we may not always agree on an interpretation, we manage to work things out satisfactorily in the end.'

1990 looked – if possible – to be an even busier year. In February Julian made a recording of the Saint-Saëns Concerto No. 1 and the Honegger Concerto together with D'Indy's *Lied* (a first recording), Fauré's *Elégie* and Saint-Saëns' *Allegro Appassionato* with the English Chamber Orchestra conducted by Yan Pascal Tortelier. Anna Barry who produced the recording for Philips was immediately impressed by Julian's single-mindedness: 'It was Julian's idea to make it with Yan Pascal Tortelier because of the association with his late father. This is the way that Julian thinks. There must always be a reason for doing things.' Julian had talked with Yan Pascal who remembered his father's pupils coming to the house and listening to his remarks while he was teaching them these concertos. Julian says: 'The Honegger Concerto was in Yan Pascal's blood: these are the things that are important to me.'

Barry, who as a Philips producer had made numerous recordings with leading musicians such as André Previn, José Carreras and Kiri Te Kanawa, was nevertheless amazed at the concentration Julian showed when re-takes were necessary. 'I have never known any other musician who can repeat a phrase or a whole section with such a high level of consistency.'

That August Julian was off on a tour of Japan, Hong Kong, Taiwan and Singapore with the Asian Youth Orchestra and Menuhin. Once again for Julian it was another fruitful collaboration with the great musician. However, in Tokyo, Menuhin's dependence on his wife, Diana, caused a problem. Menuhin insisted upon Diana being present at every performance yet, on this particular day, she had gone shopping and been caught in a traffic jam of Tokyo proportions. With the concert due to begin, there was no sign of Diana. Menuhin was adamant that he would not start unless she had arrived. No amount of persuasion would work, so with the audience and orchestra seated and the soloist waiting in the wings, there was a tense twenty-five minutes before Diana arrived and the concert was finally allowed to begin.

Yet another major Australian tour took place the following month, this time with the Australian Chamber Orchestra under Richard Hickox. The first concert was held in Sydney Opera House – a difficult place for the cello to 'carry' – but as Laurie Strachan from the *Australian* wrote: 'There was never any problem here as Lloyd Webber made his stately way through Haydn's Concerto in C major, producing a wealth of beautiful sound.'[55] Fred Blanks in the *Sydney Morning Herald* was also enthusiastic: 'His technique is superb, and there is a sense of eagarness, a swinging freshness in his delivery during fast movements which is mesmeric. To the adagio he brought strong contrasts in dynamics, making it unusually romantic. The whole approach was one to make us sit up and take notice.'[56]

*

All the while Julian had been working on a disc that would at last bring him together with his brother's music. *Lloyd Webber plays Lloyd Webber* included fifteen hits from Andrew's musicals. It was released in October and the publicity machine moved into gear. Julian appeared on *Wogan* (presented by Sue Lawley) with Bill Wyman from the Rolling Stones. Sue asked how much practice he did each day to which he replied: 'Four to six hours.' She then asked Bill the same question and Julian recalls with some amusement the horrified expression on his face when he mumbled: 'I'm lucky if I do four or five minutes.'

When *Lloyd Webber plays Lloyd Webber* was released in America, Octavio Roca of the *Washington Times* reviewed it alongside the Saint-Saëns and Honegger recording. He had no reservations about the latter and deemed it 'a source of immense pleasure'. As for *Lloyd Webber plays Lloyd Webber* he maintained, 'Julian Lloyd Webber feels the pulse of brother Andrew's music. This is one case where composer and musician breathe the same air...I confess that their coming together on this record will be a guilty pleasure for a long time.'[57]

Soon after the *Lloyd Webber plays Lloyd Webber* disc was released a concert was scheduled at the Royal Festival Hall when Andrew's *Requiem* would be performed in the second half and, before the interval, Julian would play the Elgar Concerto. The orchestra was the Royal Philharmonic with Menuhin conducting. Julian knew that Andrew would be there, but he also knew – as only brothers can – that as soon as the last note of the concerto had been sounded he would rush off to the bar. Julian asked Andrew's wife Madeleine to try to keep him in his seat as he would be playing 'John 19:41' from *Jesus Christ Superstar* as a surprise encore. Afterwards she told Julian that Andrew was moved to tears.

Chapter 10

Short Sharp Shocks

Around this time Julian embarked on a curious diversion from his unremitting concert schedule. He collected together a selection of his favourite horror stories – calling the anthology *Short Sharp Shocks*. 'My father was the one who introduced me to horror,' says Julian. 'As a boy he played cinema-organ for silent movies and was brought up on films like *Nosferatu* and *The Phantom of the Opera*. I have always enjoyed psychological horror stories – for what can be more horrific than human behaviour itself when that thin dividing line, which we think we know so well, wavers ever so slightly! As my attention span is short, I prefer reading short stories to novels and, on my plane journeys, I must have read literally thousands. I discovered that a lot of the best stories were by comparatively unknown writers. Conrad Hill was one of them and he was the one who asked the publishers, Weidenfeld & Nicholson, if they might be interested in my editing a collection. Although they said yes, I think they were more at home with political biographies than horror extravaganzas and *Short Sharp Shocks* hardly sold any copies at all. It remains an obscure little volume but, who knows, one day it may rise up from the grave!'

In September 1991 Julian returned to studio, this time joining forces with Maxim Shostakovich, conducting the London Symphony Orchestra. Together they recorded Nikolai Miaskovsky's Cello Concerto for the first time since Rostropovich's pioneering 1957 account. The disc also included Maxim's father Dimitri's *The Limpid Stream* and Tchaikovsky's *Rococo Variations* in its original version. Julian aims to get to the roots of any piece of music he performs and here again his thinking was to make the most direct contact possible with the composers: 'You could see the memories come flooding back for Maxim – he even remembered Miaskovsky coming round to his father's house for tea! These are the kind of links that can give the interpretation an extra dimension. Maxim had the ability to turn the LSO into a Russian-sounding orchestra. At the climax of the Miaskovsky, there is a series of repeated brass chords. Maxim made them sound like the revolution had just triumphed!'

Anna Barry, the record producer, has worked with Julian over many years and says: 'He never makes a compromise on the quality of performance and his intonation is always perfect. Julian also has a lot of insight into the way things work. He has an interest in every aspect of the project and what the integral elements are. He's not one of those artists who are only interested in their own part. Sadly, in my experience, this is a rare occurrence.'

For Julian, the most exciting event of 1992 was the birth of his son, David, on 25 February. In his first marriage neither he nor Celia had felt the need to have children. Now Julian will always be grateful to Zohra that she insisted on having a child. Julian recounts with pride the day when David heard him practising the Dvořák Concerto for the first time. 'He was four years old. I asked him what he thought about it; he replied, "It's so beautiful that if all the people in Afghanistan were to hear it, I think they'd stop fighting." If only the world would listen to its children.'

That autumn, Julian's recording of the Elgar Concerto with Menuhin was chosen by Jerrold Northrop Moore in *BBC Music Magazine's* 'Building a Library' feature as the 'best ever recorded version'. While Moore gives full credit to the classic 1928 recording with Beatrice Harrison conducted by the composer, he goes on to discuss the modern versions and finally determines that: 'Julian Lloyd Webber's recording matches fine performance with equally fine sound. It offers a unique link with Elgar in the conducting of Yehudi Menuhin, the last remaining active musician who was closely associated with Elgar and his world. Menuhin has deeply absorbed the delicate colours and fundamental innocence of Elgar's private world from his own experience of the man, and Julian Lloyd Webber has the musical insight to match him.' Northrop Moore concludes: 'Of all modern versions, it is Julian Lloyd Webber's performance on Philips coupled with Menuhin's deeply sensitive account of Elgar's *Enigma Variations* that wins my prize. Despite the occasional close recording of the solo cello, here is a performance to live with.'[58]

Later, Northrop Moore wrote that Julian 'brings to the concerto a profound response to Elgar's love of the earth and its seasons, the sense of man as a part of those seasons, and hence of Elgar's melancholy – though a melancholy lit with a thousand relevant lights.'[59]

Beatrice Harrison – whose early recording of the Elgar had also been singled out by Moore – was one of the first British cellists to achieve an international reputation. She was the first female cellist to play in Carnegie Hall and also a firm supporter of contemporary composers, premièring important works by Delius, Bax, Grainger, Kodály and Honegger. Julian decided there should be a centenary concert in her memory and, with considerable assistance from Beatrice's sister Margaret, it took place on 9 December 1992 at the Wigmore Hall. The programme included sonatas by Britten, John Ireland, and Delius and the Adagio from Elgar's Cello

Concerto. There was also a piece that no programme on Harrison could omit – the *Chant Hindou* by Rimsky-Korsakov. This was the music with which Beatrice Harrison hit the headlines of the time when she played her cello 'in duet' with a nightingale. She had gone into the wood at the bottom of her garden with her cello on a summer night and begun to play the *Chant Hindou*. Suddenly she heard a nightingale echoing her notes. She repeated the duet night after night and subsequently persuaded the Director of the BBC, Sir John Reith, to send a team of engineers to their home to relay the phenomenon. It was the BBC's first ever 'live' broadcast.

When Beatrice Harrison's rediscovered autobiography *The Cello and the Nightingales* was published in 1985, Julian wrote the foreword: 'Beatrice's playing was blessed with a wonderful spontaneity of phrasing and great natural facility. But what, I suspect, so beguiled and tempted those nightingales, and made her playing so very special for the rest of us, was that rapture, beauty, adoration, wonder...call it what you will, which Beatrice Harrison possessed in such rare abundance.'[60]

For Julian, organising the Beatrice Harrison concert was a labour of love: 'The two cellists who have had the most influence on me, apart from my teacher Douggie Cameron, are Rostropovich and Beatrice Harrison. Yet, except that they both play with tremendous emotion, as artists, they are chalk and cheese. Harrison at her best was a very moving player and took things emotionally to the absolute limit. Technically she wasn't perfect and she used a great deal of portamento, which people find hard to take today. But, for me her playing was so musical that it transcends any technical shortcomings.'

In February 1993 Julian made his début at the Salzburg Mozarteum with John Lenehan in the programme of music by Fauré, Rachmaninov and Britten. Julian was suffering from a heavy cold and was also nervous at appearing for the first time in Mozart's birthplace. But he remembers that his 'blocked sinus and splitting headache' helped him forget his nerves. The critics were certainly impressed: 'The splendour of the evening's recital lay in the fabulously beautiful sound of the instrument which Julian Lloyd Webber knew how to use throughout its range – perfect changes of register, convincing bowing technique and, above all, precise intonation characterised the playing of the secure expert, an attitude intensified by his combination of brilliance and depth of feeling.'[61]

Next day, Julian's problems began. He was due to play the Brahms Clarinet Trio in a lunchtime concert at the South Bank with John Lill and Emma Johnson. When he arrived at Salzburg airport the flight to Heathrow had been cancelled and the next flight would only just make it to London in time. Julian had no option but to practise the cello part of the trio in the airport lounge and he arrived on the concert platform with moments to spare. These occurrences are daily hazards in the life of a travelling musician but, if Julian is asked what is the most nerve-wracking experience, he will join the large number of performers who dread broadcasting 'live' on the radio. Not only are they totally dependent on the whims of the engineers for ensuring balance and sound that comes across, but the listener at home remains blissfully unaware of the atmosphere in the concert hall.

Julian vividly remembers an occasion when he was giving a lunch-time recital for BBC Radio 3 from the Bradford Library Theatre. Admission was free to all these concerts: 'a policy that was doubtless very encouraging to music lovers who cannot afford high ticket prices, but it also resulted in some very strange characters wandering in for a temporary escape from the prevailing elements.' On this occasion, no sooner had he embarked upon the ethereal slow movement of Beethoven's D major Sonata – one of the deepest (and quietest) in music – than a somewhat bedraggled lady tramp shambled into the theatre muttering all the while, and set off down the gangway towards the platform. Settling herself noisily in the front row, she pulled from her pocket a packet of crisps. Julian recalls: 'Each time the music paused – pregnant with meaning – I was deafened by the crunch of her salt'n'vinegars. Surely I would have to stop – her antics must be ruining the broadcast. But I had a nagging suspicion that this nasty incident would be going by unnoticed over the air and that an outburst about crisps would seem strangely inappropriate. I soldiered on. Sure enough, when I got home and listened to the tape, the cacophony hadn't registered.'

By 1993, Julian had celebrated 21 years as a soloist but somehow the spectre of living in his brother's shadow had never left him. In a perceptive article by Andrew Stewart in *Classical Music*, Julian made his feelings clear. When asked if he had ever attempted to profit from his family connection or raise his own public profile to match that of his brother's, he was emphatic. 'One thing that I know for a fact is that there is no way a classical musician should compete with that in terms of publicity. You have to be your own man. There have been times when over-zealous recording companies have tried to capitalise on the link with Andrew and I'm convinced that was a mistake. Trivialisation of classical music in order to get a story is unsafe. You can understand why people trying to sell classical music do that sort of thing, but I don't think it is helpful to the music at all.'

Julian makes it clear that one of the main problems is that the popular press are only interested in the size of Pavarotti's girth or Vanessa Mae's cleavage and he maintains that musicians in the 'serious' field are undervalued in a way that never seems to apply to pop stars or sportsmen.

He also resents the way that the press latch on to anything out of the ordinary and blow it up out of all proportion. He cites the time in the early eighties when he did a few concerts with Stephane Grappelli: 'There was a blaze of publicity, which was not particularly sought after. It was because I was doing something that wasn't *classical*. When a classical musician plays classical music there is no press attention. I think that's unfortunate because it encourages classical musicians to do attention-grabbing things.'

In common with many of his fellow musicians and music lovers, Julian would like to bring classical music to a wider audience but the danger is that, when the media begin to interfere, they trivialise and do not seem interested unless there is some 'sensationalist' story attached. Julian remarked: 'For every classical musician who makes it big in the *Sun*, tens of thousands languish in relative obscurity. This can be a possible incentive for young players to imitate the antics of "Nige" or to conform to what looks and sounds like a marketable package.'[62]

March 1993 brought an extended tour of America with the 'Moscow Soloists,' playing the Haydn C major Concerto. (The 'Moscow Soloists' were initially set up by the viola player Yuri Bashmet when he was still living in the USSR.) When the tour of fourteen concerts was arranged, Julian was told they had organised a coach that was fitted up with a bed for him on the overnight trips. Julian was not too happy about the coach situation and told the management, Columbia Artists, that he had decided to fly and would join them at the various hotels. He soon realised that the road travel was, in many instances, quicker and the coach often arrived first. 'By the time I had arrived at the various airports, suffered from flight delays and the slow speed of the "Fokkers" that are used on some of the internal flights, I often arrived late.' Julian enjoyed working with these superb musicians, but his indelible memory of the trip was of the vast amount of hard liquor consumed that seemed to be a way of life for the musicians. 'Every night after the concert they would go to one of their hotel rooms and imbibe an amount of vodka that was unbelievable. Yet the next morning they would be bright and smiling, ready for the day's coach trip.'

That autumn, Julian's recording *Cradle Song* was released. It came about because the birth of his son, David, the previous year had inspired him to become the third member of the family to compose. He explains: 'Six weeks after my son David was born I was spending a typical afternoon at home practising. Only one thing was very different; the tiny body of my little boy lay sleeping quietly beside me. For the first time in my life I started to compose. A tune, a lullaby, came to me quickly and easily.'

Typically, from this moment Julian's lively imagination began to wonder about music that had been inspired by children. He unearthed a wealth of material and the idea of making a recording developed. Julian said: '*Cradle Song* will, almost certainly, be my most personal recording, yet its inspiration – the innocence of childhood – is universal and timeless.'

Besides his own *Song for Baba* and a *Slumber Song* by his father, there are lullabies from a wide variety of composers from Schumann, Schubert, Brahms and Fauré to Roger Quilter, Khachaturian and Richard Rodney Bennett, who composed a special 'Dream Sequence' based on film music for children for the recording. *Gramophone* commented that although the pieces are all in the 'same, slowish-paced, lyrical vein... their sequence has been cleverly chosen so that there is plenty of variety to keep the listener's attention,' and continued: 'Throughout the programme Julian Lloyd Webber plays with exceptional sensitivity, sympathy and tonal beauty – in fact it would be difficult to find better performances of this kind of repertoire anywhere on records of today or yesterday.'[63]

As an interesting afterthought to *Cradle Song*, Julian

contacted Richard Rodney Bennett to see if he would be interested in writing a concerto based on Hollywood themes. Bennett declined, saying that he had no interest in film music – a surprising response from the composer of the scores for *Murder on the Orient Express* and *Four Weddings and a Funeral*.

After his father's death, Julian became closer to his mother than he had ever been. He knew that her cancer was spreading, but she never complained and was always ready to listen to whatever news he had to tell her. As the years went by the relationship developed in a way he would never have visualised – especially when he looked back on the rather distant person she had been when he and his brother were children. Julian would often practise in her flat and tell her about everything that was going on – something that would have been unthinkable years before. He remembers that she loved gossip, especially when it concerned her sons' matrimonial difficulties. She would pretend to be shocked at the various happenings, but in reality she enjoyed the intrigues enormously and would sometimes comment with a sense of humour that Julian had not realised she possessed.

Eventually Jean's cancer spread to such an extent that in October of that year she was forced to have an operation. At first it was thought to have been successful. But it was only a minimal reprieve and within a month the cancer had returned, worse than ever. Julian spent time with her every day and knew that the end must come soon.

Meanwhile he had been booked for many concerts that had to be fulfilled. The most important was at Amsterdam's beautiful Concertgebouw Hall. He was to play one of his favourite concertos, the Shostakovich No. 1. The concert was on a Monday and he had to travel to Amsterdam on the previous Sunday evening. Julian visited his mother in hospital on Sunday morning and it was clear that she was dying. He said he would prefer to cancel the concert but Jean was adamant. 'Don't you dare cancel! If you do, I'll never forgive you.' With a heavy heart Julian left for Amsterdam, knowing that he would never see his mother again.

Several critics – who knew nothing of his sadness – said that it was particularly moving, especially the slow movement which has a long, slow cadenza right in the middle lasting almost ten minutes. 'My mother was very much on my mind throughout. I felt she was with me.' Jean died just a few hours after he had finished playing and the hospital telephoned his hotel in the middle of the night leaving a message which he did not get until the morning. Afterwards Julian said: 'On the one hand, I had just done something that was very important for me, and on the other my mother had died.'

Everyone who knew Jean well said that she was 'psychic'. She had written a letter to Julian, which he found when he collected her belongings from the hospital. In the note – amongst other things – she said she would try to make her presence felt. According to the nurse, at the moment of her 'death' she appeared to be looking intently at something that made her smile. Her last words were: 'So it *is* true.'

Julian feels that although, physically, both his parents are no longer here, they remain very close to him. 'I've always felt that they are still here with me. Now there is just Andrew and me – there is no older generation of any kind. Suddenly you realise that you are the only ones carrying the torch, and it does bring you closer together.'[64]

Julian's work on his father's manuscripts had resulted in several CDs. *Invocation* was particularly memorable: 'A tremendous amount of work went into that recording. The manuscripts and the orchestral parts had to be prepared and the actual recording was a very strange experience for me. I was hearing these pieces played for the first time and discovering just what my father was all about – in front of these fine musicians! *Lento for Strings* is an extraordinary work: the earliest piece on the disc, it is harmonically the most advanced and shows the direction my father could have taken had he wished.' Richard Hickox confirmed: 'There is no doubt that this is evidence of what a brilliant composer he was.' Certainly *Aurora* is everything that Andrew has described and *Invocation* is another gem – emotional, melancholic but in good taste and innately musical. Richard Hickox recalls that Julian was doggedly persistent in his single-handed efforts to bring his father's music back to life. 'I do so admire him for all the hard work he put into this project. He was also quite right in his belief that the music was written by a first-class composer. I was astonished when I first read some of the scores. I think William Lloyd Webber is very underrated and Julian has done a spectacular job in making his music available.'

Chapter 11

Farewell to Philosophy

In January 1994 Julian and John Lenehan gave a recital at the Jewish Community Center in Rockville, USA, and Mark Carrington's review in the *Washington Post* must have been music to Julian's ears: 'With more than 30 recordings to his credit, cellist Julian Lloyd Webber need never fear about living in his brother Andrew's shadow. And while concert artists rarely win mass acclaim – and of the few that do, still fewer are cellists – Julian Lloyd Webber's star shines brightly in that small constellation of the deserving few.' He then comments on the 'fine touch and keen intellect' which he and Lenehan brought to their performance: 'Architecture was always in place, and each piece on this most challenging program (Bach, Debussy, Fauré and Rachmaninov) conveyed a sense of journey, of departure and arrival.' He concludes that they: 'evinced the skills and vision to make the music memorable even when, in the case of the Rachmaninov Sonata and the Frank Bridge encore, neglect might have consigned them to a different fate.'[65]

When Julian's recording *English Idyll*, with the Academy of St Martin in the Fields conducted by Sir Neville Marriner, was released it received glowing praise from almost every critic. Julian was in his element with rarely heard music by Delius, John Ireland, Elgar, Grainger, Vaughan Williams and others.

Time Out called it 'English music at its most yearningly pastoral, evoking a mixture of nostalgia and dreamy regret. I'm a sucker for it.'[66] Michael Quinn in *The Lady* was unstinting in his recommendation. 'If there is a more sensitive performer of the cello in this country or a more imaginative and intelligent programmer of its repertoire than Julian Lloyd Webber, he has yet to make himself known...this is the perfect gift for those who love wonderful music wonderfully played.'[67] Michael Kennedy in the *Sunday Telegraph* makes it Critic's Choice: 'Julian Lloyd Webber is in persuasive form...Lovely performances.'[68] *Classic FM* says: 'Lloyd Webber loves this music – and it shows.'[69] *Stereo Review* writes about 'exemplary performances throughout.'[70] The obvious rapport between conductor and soloist is confirmed by Sir Neville Marriner who had found Julian 'always most agreeable to work with – interpretatively flexible, technically unpretentious and musically generous.'[71]

Julian's interpretations are aptly characterised by Jerrold Northrop Moore: 'To achieve the personal balances Julian does all the time in his performances needs the intellect to set creator and performer in proper perspective, insight *and technique* to keep the performance true to the music; and great courage to follow a self-abnegating course in the face of insistent vulgarising fashion. It is a quality I associate with the finest aspect of traditional English character.'[72]

On a return visit to the USA in May Julian played the original version of the Tchaikovsky *Rococo Variations* at the Florida Philharmonic 'Proms', conducted by James Judd. James Roos in the *Miami Herald* was obviously bowled over by a performance he found 'so exquisite it will remain indelible.' He continued:

In decades of concert-going, I've become a hopelessly spoiled aisle-sitter. I can virtually recall the *Rococo Variations* played incisively by such cellists as Pierre

Fournier, André Navarra, Antonio Janigro, Leonard Rose, Mstislav Rostropovich – and, not so long ago with the Florida Philharmonic, Janos Starker. But never have I heard the intimate character of this masterwork more eloquently drawn and penetrated than by Julian Lloyd Webber.

Not only is he a superlative cellist with seemingly effortless technique, but he also is a *marvellous* musician who pays keen attention to tender tone coloring. He can turn fluted harmonics into the wispiest filaments of tone, and he knows all about this work as a Tchaikovskian salute to Mozart. Each variation sounded freshly minted – in fact one variation traditionally omitted since the first performance by Fitzenhagen in 1877 was restored here so that the old horse sounded even newer. A deserved standing ovation coaxed Lloyd Webber into a poignant encore; the first movement of the Malcolm Arnold *Fantasy*.'[73]

Julian's assistant at the time was Callum Ross and, between tours, they were hard at work unearthing Bill's music. Ross remembers: 'One of the major problems faced by Julian when collating his father's music was to find out precisely its whereabouts and with whom copyright rested. William Lloyd Webber composed a wide variety of music for a wide variety of publishers, a number of whom had subsequently either gone out of business or been taken over.'

Despite this, Julian continued his researches: 'As a result I finally came to realise just how much music he had written. I knew about *Aurora* because of the old recording, and of course there were the pieces we included in that first CD. But I didn't think there was much more. Now there are *five* CDs – two of which Callum helped me to bring about – and together we tracked down all the published music amounting to sixty works. Two pieces remain lost – a *Benedictus* for Strings and a *Nocturne* for Piano and Strings.'

Ross remembers that he was often surprised by the

music's unpredictability: 'A melodic or harmonic sequence which, within less gifted hands, would have taken a perfectly acceptable but conventional route was crafted to follow an original one, without sounding contrived.'[74]

With so much music uncovered Julian decided there ought at last to be a concert devoted to William Lloyd Webber's music. The story of how it happened is best told by Pam Chowhan who was at the time responsible for programming the Lunchtime Concert Series in the South Bank's Purcell Room. 'I really wanted Julian to perform in the series, and we struck a deal whereby he would give a concert, if he had total choice over his programme. He chose to perform a concert solely of his father's music, with John Lill as his accompanist.' She had to check up with various superiors who were naturally wary of putting on a concert devoted entirely to the music of a completely unknown composer. Finally, they were persuaded and it was arranged for 9 February 1995. To Julian's surprise there was a great deal of interest prior to the concert and on the day it was absolutely packed. In fact people were queuing in the hope of returns. Chowhan recalls: 'I had never seen such a long queue at one of my lunch-time concerts.' Julian remembers: 'After all the mystery surrounding my father's music, I just couldn't believe it was happening.'

The critics were impressed, and not only by the packed hall. Malcolm Hayes in the *Daily Telegraph* remarked on the way in which modernism had dominated the sixties thus silencing Lloyd Webber's 'creative voice', and added: 'He was not the only one whose music was kicked into touch by committee-room dictators in those thankfully long-gone days.' Hayes went on to praise his skill as a miniaturist and extols his rare gift of 'setting up and rounding off a satisfying musical statement in a short space of time.' He points out that Lloyd Webber was known to be an admirer of Rachmaninov and he concluded: 'Perhaps the Russian composer's example lies behind Lloyd Webber's ultra-compressed Scherzo in G minor and almost as terse Arabesque. In both cases the piano writing flickers with haunting brilliance that lingers in the memory as far too much 20th century music does not. It is high time we heard more of this unpretentious and intriguing musical voice. And not just in the Purcell Room at lunch-time.'[75]

Pam Chowhan was naturally delighted by the success. As a result, she thought it would be interesting to have a connecting theme running through each season of the Lunchtime Concerts. 'I always liked to bounce ideas off Julian, and I asked him what he thought about having an "English composers" theme. He inspired me with the suggestion of focusing on his father's music for the Autumn '95 season as a natural follow-on from the concert he'd just performed in February. At that time, Julian was working very hard on researching and resurrecting as much of his father's music as possible. He was indefatigable in his efforts to get it recognised, played, published (if it wasn't already) and recorded. It was a very time-consuming undertaking for him, but, I think, very close to his heart. 'Julian saw that the Lunchtime Series could provide a valuable platform for the music. The idea was that each participant in the series would include one work by William Lloyd Webber. The musicians were all very happy to accommodate this idea, and the concerts were very well received. I remember that particular venture as one of the highlights of my programming career.'

At one of the concerts, the Solomon Trio played Bill's *Fantasy Trio* and it was Matthew Rye, again in the *Daily Telegraph*, who recognised the 'distinctly personal . . . yearning, rhythmically driven melodies for the violin and cello and individually chromatic chord progressions for the piano . . . It would make an attractive addition to any trio's repertoire.'[76]

Meanwhile, Julian was hard at work on a contemporary commission. Philips – at Julian's suggestion – had asked Gavin Bryars to write a cello concerto, but commissioning a new work can be fraught with problems. What Julian had in mind was a twenty-minute piece for soloist and string orchestra that would pair comfortably in a concert alongside one of the Haydn concertos. What emerged was a thirty-seven minute work for soloist and full symphony orchestra called *Farewell to Philosophy*. Premièred at the Barbican on 24 November with the English Chamber Orchestra conducted by James Judd, it was well-received by the critics. Nicolas Williams in the *Independent* thought that the concerto was 'well fitted out to match the particular strengths' of Julian's playing, 'his warm legato in particular.'[77] Tim Ashley in the *Guardian* thought the concerto 'both elusive and allusive, and demands repeated hearings,' adding that 'Lloyd Webber plays with great fervour and remarkable variety of expression, given there is little to demand in virtuosity.'[78]

When the CD with the concerto and other works by Bryars was released, the reviews were also encouraging. The *Gramophone* critic not only liked the concerto itself but thought that Julian's tone was 'perfectly suited to the job, being full-blooded and expressive but relaxed enough to blend with the components of a predominantly dark accompaniment.'[79] The *Evening Standard*'s reviewer, Alexander Waugh, had a long memory for he singled out the way in which Julian 'sings its long lines with the same plaintive intensity that marked his extraordinary recording of the Delius Cello Concerto over a decade ago. It is a gently haunting work which reveals abundant new secrets each time you hear it.'[80] *The Strad* magazine was also impressed: 'The chief delight is Julian Lloyd Webber's intelligent reading of the solo line – beautifully judged and sustained, gorgeous in tone, subtle in nuance and utterly disarming in the final Farewell, which really does feel like a culmination. Lloyd Webber also underlines how, within Bryars, there lies both a refreshing honesty and an unashamed English Romantic.'[81]

Chapter 12

Mazdamania

1996 did not start well for Julian. He was suffering from a recurrent 'flu bug that made him feel listless most of the time. He saw several doctors, all of whom offered remedies that did nothing to help. Nonetheless he battled on giving concerts including one at the Hong Kong Festival playing the Dvořák Concerto with the German NDR Symphony Orchestra.

After several months, he was saved by Dr Brian Piggott, who had been a partner of Julian's uncle. He made a number of tests and finally came up with the right antibiotic. It was just in time to enable Julian to record of the Britten Cello Symphony and the Walton Concerto with Neville Marriner and the Academy of St Martin in the Fields, which was scheduled for June at Watford Town Hall.

In August Julian travelled to Stockholm to give a recital of the complete cello works of Delius and Grieg with the pianist Bengt Forsberg. The partnership with Forsberg came about through a typical piece of Julian planning to 'get to the roots': 'I knew he was a specialist in the Scandinavian song repertoire and he has worked through much of it with Anne-Sophie von Otter. He also has a reputation for exploring unusual music so I went to hear them in recital at the Wigmore Hall and was enormously impressed. Bengt has a lot to offer, interpretatively as well as musically. He isn't someone who just accompanies. I wanted to take advantage of that expertise so I approached him to make a recording. He runs a recital series in Stockholm so that's where we played all the pieces that are on our CD. But we didn't just make a disc – we played and worked together extensively before we did the recording.' Forsberg and Julian then gave a Wigmore Hall recital themselves in September of that year.

March 1997, saw Julian as a co-soloist with John Harle at the Royal Festival Hall in Michael Nyman's Double Concerto for Cello and Saxophone. It sounded an interesting experiment but the project got off to a bad start with the advance publicity. The concerto had been commissioned by the Japanese car manufacturers Mazda, who wanted Nyman to write a piece that celebrated Mazda but also related to the dreadful happenings during the war at Hiroshima, where their factory is based. Although Nyman accepted the commission, it was soon apparent that he was not happy with Mazda's suggestions and simply wanted to write a concerto for cello and saxophone which, in itself, was a novel idea.

Once the press discovered the disagreement between Nyman and Mazda they had a field day and, in Julian's view, the concerto was 'up against it' from that point.

The performance was marred by bad amplification and the cello could only be heard when Julian had the opportunity to play a phrase or two completely solo. Andrew, who came to the première, was not enamoured and expressed himself in no uncertain terms afterwards and this soon reached the composer's ears. 'Londoner's Diary' in the *Evening Standard* noted: 'When Nyman's new Concerto for Saxophone and Cello was premièred recently at the Royal Festival Hall, Julian Lloyd Webber – a very distinguished soloist – took one of the solo parts. And Lord Andrew Lloyd Webber came along, naturally, to provide fraternal support. But his lordship did not enjoy the evening one bit. "He thought it sounded like *Riverdance*," Nyman told me tersely.' When Andrew was telephoned he was diplomacy itself. He regretted not being able to hear his brother properly but could not recall what else he had said.[82] Julian's account of the events leading up to the first performance is self-explanatory: 'The manuscript was very late in arriving and I was getting bits of it by fax the week before. The first rehearsal was on the afternoon before the concert and, when we reached the first section where there is a change of time, Nyman suddenly stopped everyone and said "Sorry, boys. I think I've got this wrong. It shouldn't say crochet = 60, it should be crochet = 120." So suddenly we had to play everything at twice the speed we had been practising!'

Critically, it would be difficult to find a première that had a worse reception. The *Guardian* thought the piece was 'fraught with ambiguity... and immediately suggests the hijacking of artistic integrity for the purpose of advertising expensive cars.' It continued: 'The real problem is that Nyman's orchestral writing lacks assurance. The quirky transparent textures of music written for his own band clot and cloy when transferred to a Mahler-sized orchestra. The soloists are dangerously out of balance, with Julian Lloyd Webber frequently inaudible (despite massive amplification) against the density of the orchestral sound.'[83] *The Times* was even more scathing: 'The pulse is pumped out with steely virtuosity. The amplification is oppressive; the orchestration unremittingly thick. Nuance, charm and wit are absent; the beat goes on, and literally has no time for such incidental delights.' And Julian: 'could be seen digging his bow furiously into his strings, but [was] rarely heard.'[84]

The *Observer* had a head-start; as their critic was obviously not a Nyman fan:

It was commissioned by the car company Mazda, and didn't we know it... The new concerto opens quietly, with the two soloists together singing a slow lamenting line of no immediate promise. That is about as subtle as the work gets. Soon we are back to familiar Nyman territory – soprano saxophone and a horribly over-amplified cello closely following each other and screaming over dense unremitting textures, aggressively repeated orchestral chords and naïve, painfully slow, harmonic changes. The piece is, ultimately, as dour, dogged, unpoetic, unimaginative, unsurprising, insensitive, and emotionally uninvolved as most Nyman.'[85]

It was Tully Potter in *The Strad* who rendered the ultimate criticism: 'The amplification had the effect of making a Strad cello sound like a wheezing wind instrument much of the time. Nyman appears to have about three musical ideas in his head, all of the utmost banality, and he alternates them *ad nauseum*. At the time of writing, Nyman has failed to deliver his Viola Concerto on time for Tabea Zimmerman. I wonder if he could be persuaded to hang on to it until, I, at least, am dead and in no danger of hearing it.'[86]

The resultant CD, made at Abbey Road, seems to have benefited from the expertise of the sound engineers. Writing in the *Observer* Fiona Maddocks said: 'Nyman's inimitable sound may not win new converts with this disc, but no one can deny its skill, high energy and snatches of exquisite melody. At the première of the Sax and Cello Concerto, complaints were made that the cello could not be heard. With the benefit of a well-balanced recording, Lloyd Webber's cello sings eloquently with Harle's smooth sax. Nyman structures his work tightly and makes thoughtful play of the concerto form. He is also blessed with top soloists.'[87]

Julian agrees that the concerto works a lot better on disc, but even the recording was fraught with problems: 'When it came to making the CD, Nyman wanted to conduct, but the orchestra was pre-recorded and – two weeks later – we tracked the saxophone and cello parts on top with Michael in attendance. But he was busy writing a new score at the time.

Suddenly, as we were listening to the playback, he looked up and said: "How can I compose with all this ____ing racket going on!" '

By contrast on 11 June, Julian took part in a moving historical occasion. He had been invited to play the Elgar Concerto in one of two celebratory concerts with Sir Neville Marriner and the Academy of St Martin in the Fields to mark the Hong Kong changeover to Chinese rule at the Hong Kong Arts Centre. Nigel Kennedy played Elgar's Violin Concerto at the other concert. The British Governor, Chris Patten, was there along with many other political dignitaries. Anthony Camden, the Director of the Hong Kong Academy of Music (and the eldest son of the great bassoonist, Archie Camden) had suggested Marriner and the ASMF for the occasion. Sir Neville recalls: 'Both Julian and Nigel Kennedy made memorable performances of the two concertos, as befitted the importance of the occasion,' and adds, 'Julian has always generated extraordinary expectation from his audiences, and this was no exception.'[88]

Julian remembers the occasion for two reasons. 'After David was born it was one of the few foreign tours when Zohra accompanied me and I was so happy that she was there. The concert itself was held on the very night before the changeover and the atmosphere in the hall was quite extraordinary – a totally special happening. We had the Elgar in the first half and it was the end of an era. In the second half there was a Chinese piece and that was it: British music was out – Chinese music was in. Although it seemed a sad occasion, it was one of the most memorable concerts of my life.'

Certainly Julian's other collaboration with Sir Neville and the ASMF (on the Walton Concerto and Britten Cello Symphony) had resulted on one of his finest recordings to date. Sir Neville sums it up in one sentence: 'In the recording studio Julian performs with remarkable consistency.' Without exception, the critics raved. An 'Editor's Choice' in

Gramophone, Edward Greenfield enthused: 'Not only is the power of each piece fully laid out, the beauty is presented as never before on disc... This is the finest, most formidable disc that Julian Lloyd Webber has yet given us.'[89] In *Classic CD* Malcolm Hayes wrote: 'not since Rostropovich has Britten's Cello Symphony been so masterfully played. Lloyd Webber's sound is wonderfully true, accurate, and gloss-free, so that the notes really speak for themselves.'[90] The *Independent on Sunday* has Michael White running out of superlatives: 'no-one plays more beautifully or with more commitment.'[91] Michael Kennedy, selecting it as 'Critic's Choice' in the *Sunday Telegraph*, wrote about 'heart-warming perception' of contrasting values, and: 'his interpretation of the first movement of the Britten in some respects penetrates deeper into its morosely elegiac musings than Rostropovich's.'[92]

Many other national newspapers reviewed the recording in similar vein, often comparing Julian's interpretation with Rostropovich. Perhaps the most interesting review came from that hypercritical critic Tully Potter in the *Daily Mail*, who began by saying that if anyone could make these two works popular, it would be Julian. 'In his own, more restrained, classical fashion, he comes even closer than Rostropovich in some ways to the quiet kind of Englishness represented by Britten. The Walton is beautifully played by both cellist and orchestra and goes straight to the top of the all-too-few recommendations for this work.'[93] Julian considers this recording to be his best so far: 'Everyone concerned contributed to its success. When the Britten was premièred in Moscow with the English Chamber Orchestra, Rostropovich was the soloist but the leader of the orchestra was Kenneth Sillitoe – who led the ASMF on our recording and the principal second violin was Sir Neville! So we had two direct links to the work's first performance.'

In July, Julian made a welcome excursion into chamber music at the Verbier Festival in Switzerland. Although he has always enjoyed playing with his fellow musicians in smaller ensembles the occasions for doing so had been few. Verbier redressed the balance with a vengeance and Julian's enthusiasm was boundless: 'It was a wonderfully exciting experience in a beautiful setting with great company. All the musicians took masterclasses as well, which I found rewarding, but it was the spirit of cameraderie among the players that was unforgettable.

'One morning I was walking in the street and the violinist Dimitri Sitkovetsky, who was sitting in a café, signalled me to join him. It seemed that they had a problem in that someone who had promised to play the Mendelssohn Octet was not well, so could I join them? Others in the group included "Jimmy" (Cho-Liang) Lin and Julian Rachlin. Then I played the Dvořák Piano Quintet in a group with Dimitri and his mother, the pianist Bella Davidovich. Another high spot was Villa-Lobos' *Bachianas Brasileiras* No. 5 for eight cellos and soprano with a group that included David Geringas, Mischa Maisky and Natalie Clein with Barbara Hendricks as the soloist.'

Sadly, Julian's old friend Eric Fenby had died earlier that year. Julian had been closely associated with this man who had shared the last few years of Delius's life when the composer was blind, paralysed and living in his retreat in rural France. On 16 September, the Delius Society gave a Memorial Concert at the Wigmore Hall and Julian played the Cello Sonata with John Lenehan. Matthew Rye from the *Daily Telegraph* thought that the duo had performed the Sonata 'with the same devotion and ardour they had given the work during the City of London Festival in July, their phrasing wonderfully controlled and shaped.'[94] *The Strad* was also impressed. Joanne Talbot commented that they had perfectly captured the concept of the music 'producing a great intensity in the Cello Sonata that completely captured the audience.'[95]

Following the Fenby Memorial concert, the BBC presented one of their *Vintage Years* programmes on Radio 3, devised and introduced by David Mellor, in which a distinguished musician from the present time is invited to talk about a great artist from the past. Alfred Brendel talked about Edwin Fischer, Bernard Haitink talked about Mengelberg and Julian was invited to give his appreciation of his former teacher Pierre Fournier. David Mellor explained why he chose Julian: 'Julian's interest in music is very widespread and his explorations are not a question of egotism on his part. He can talk lucidly and intelligently about his art. The way he spoke about Fournier was the voice of the true enthusiast. He was loving hearing his recordings and pointing out what was good about them. His was an exceptionally good programme and no one who listened to it could have failed to emerge with not only a greater appreciation of the art of Fournier, but also of Julian's enthusiasm. And this, by the way, is not something that the record company had said would get his name better known so that people would go out and buy his discs. He was so honest. I recall that Fournier played a concerto by Boccherini and Julian said: "It's a pity I can't play that concerto because today you would have to play it with an authentic instrument ensemble and a baroque cello with gut strings and I regret that I am not into this movement." This is typical of Julian's honesty in that there are certain parts of the repertoire that are difficult for a cellist of his generation to explore, but he still wants us to glory in Fournier's interpretation of it.'

That November Hyperion released a CD on which Julian played the very beautiful *Sapphic Poem* for Cello and Orchestra by Granville Bantock. Here we have yet another composer whose work has been sorely neglected over the years and the disc was universally welcomed by the reviewers. The *Sapphic Poem* was first heard with piano accompaniment in 1906 and Bantock's version with orchestra was published three years later. Andrew Achenbach in *Gramophone* notes its delicate scoring: 'beautifully conceived for the medium, it is a richly melodious, sweetly expressive outpouring, raptly performed here by Julian Lloyd Webber, who in turns receives exemplary support from Handley and the RPO.'[96] In *Classic CD* Julian Haylock says that Julian 'plays it as though it were one of the treasured gems of the repertoire.'[97] Joanne Talbot in *The Strad* writes of: 'the mellifluous cello melody floating above an orchestral canopy of ravishing harmonies. Meandering it may be, but given the relative brevity (fifteen minutes), I would have thought this piece might engage the imagination of other cellists. Of course, Julian Lloyd Webber has long-since found his niche in this rich English repertoire, to which he brings great sensitivity.'[98]

Professionally Julian seemed to be climbing to greater and greater heights, but his personal life was rapidly descending to the depths. His arguments with Zohra were becoming more and more frequent and, although he did not want to admit it, Julian knew that his second attempt at marriage was falling apart.

Chapter 13

East is Best

Early in 1998 Julian had two important engagements – the Canadian première of the Bryars Concerto and the Britten Cello Symphony at the Salle Pleyel in Paris. The Bryars première was in Ottawa and was well received by audience and press alike, but Julian was unprepared for the extremes of the Canadian winter. An unexpected avalanche of snow kept him a prisoner in his hotel for three days. 'I had not brought the score of the Britten with me so I couldn't even practise. We were completely snowed in and it felt like forever.'

Shortly after his performance of the Britten in Paris, Julian had an unexpected opportunity to air his opinions on important issues close to his heart. He had been invited to play Tchaikovsky's *Rococo Variations* with the European Community Youth Orchestra conducted by Ivan Fischer at the World Economic Forum at Davos in Switzerland. The organisers asked if he would like to make a ten-minute speech on any classical music related subject of his choice. At first he was hesitant, but a recent experience had set him thinking about the differences between the East and the West in their attitudes to classical music.

The previous November Julian had been in hospital for a sinus operation and was forced to stay in bed for several days. His only amusement was provided by the television: 'I watched Breakfast TV for the first time in years. Everything seemed to last about ten seconds and I started to wonder where – if anywhere – classical music could fit into all this?' So Julian decided he would speak on 'Classical Music in Western Culture Today' and he pulled no punches: 'Declining audiences, government cuts, disastrous CD sales, sponsors pulling out of the arts, fewer children learning instruments and a total lack of interest from the general media – unless semi-naked bimbo violinists or something like the David Helfgott circus are involved. This is the reality of classical music in the west today.'

He went on to say that all this was in strong contrast to music-making in the Far East where there are still vast numbers of children learning instruments, healthy classical CD sales, a media that shows real interest in classical music and – above all – 'concert halls that are packed with young people as a direct result of the media interest.' He then emphasises that we have to face the truth that the vast majority of young people in the West have 'no interest in classical music whatsoever.'

Julian feels strongly that the decline in the number of young people learning to play musical instruments not only deprives them of the pleasure that they can derive from the activity in itself, but also threatens the orchestras of the future: 'Young people are force-fed their culture by the media, especially television, and that culture is pop, pop and more pop.' He quotes *The Times* arts editor, Richard Morrison: 'Why do the arts have so few friends in the TV companies, who neither report nor cover anything vaguely "highbrow"? Why are business leaders scuttling out of sponsorship deals? Why are teachers not evangelising for the arts in their classrooms?'

Julian also acknowledges Norman Lebrecht, who expressed in his book *When the Music Stops* his view that classical music has been 'pushed to the periphery of public attention' and sets the date of the decline from the Three Tenors concert in 1990.

In his speech, Julian stated that we must look much further back 'to discover the beginnings of the current malaise and delve into an area which possibly even Mr Lebrecht found too sensitive. This particular "hornets nest" is not even mentioned in his book – despite being arguably the primary cause of classical music's alienation from its audience. I refer, of course, to contemporary music. In order to survive, music must be a living, developing art, exciting its audiences. Yet for forty years of madness – from 1945 to the early eighties – classical music turned its back on its audiences and shot itself in the foot with the result that, today, it remains seriously wounded.'

Julian goes on to bemoan the fact that instead of rebuilding the acoustically superb Queen's Hall in London, the decision was made to move out of the city centre and create an entirely new concrete structure on the south bank of the Thames. He maintains we are still paying for that mistake as neither the Royal Festival Hall nor the later Barbican Centre are acoustically comparable to the world's great concert halls. He mentions that similar concrete mausoleums were built all over the west, which hardly proved conducive to an enjoyable evening out. 'As the concert halls became more severe, so did the music itself. Suddenly it was only acceptable to write in one style. Composers who had pursued a logical development of the music of the great masters were increasingly disparaged and derided by the new *führers* of the classical music establishment, for whom tonality and harmony had become dirty words.' He is emphatic that he is not criticising that style *per se* but simply objects to the strait-jacket that it imposed upon all new compositions.

He continued: 'After the war, Western classical music created a pernicious *Politburo* that proved every bit as effective as its counterpart in the East.' He then cites the composers who were dismissed as 'dated': Aaron Copland and Samuel Barber in the US, Berthold Goldschmidt in Germany and, in England, William Walton and even

Benjamin Britten. 'Malcolm Arnold also wrote a number of symphonies and chamber works, and perhaps because he also wrote film music and dared to include humour in his writing, he faced a perpetual chorus of discouragement. When one of his finest works – the Fifth Symphony – was premièred at the 1961 Cheltenham Festival, it was described as "a creative personality in an advanced state of disintegration."

'While classical music was busy shooting itself in the foot, pop music was making huge advances. Great talents like Elvis Presley, Buddy Holly, the Beatles and the Beach Boys were providing the melody and harmony that classical music appeared to despise. In the fifties and sixties classical music broke its trust with young people. As a result it lost its relevance to the media, who decided that we were living in a pop culture. Classical music must never make that mistake again,' says Julian, because it makes it much harder for the many fine composers today like James MacMillan, John Adams and John Tavener – successful though they are – to win back the trust of audiences who are wary of contemporary music. He asks: 'Is classical music in the doldrums?' and answers 'Statistically, yes, but creatively, no. Today, there is a much healthier climate for new music as musicians and critics are willing to judge a new piece on its own terms instead of comparing it with Stockhausen. Composers, performers and orchestras are at their most inventive for years, but they cannot do it all on their own.' In his opinion, 'Western classical music is being starved to the brink of death by lack of media attention. Concerts are given nightly in our cities almost unnoticed by the newspapers, and even in the *quality* newspapers days can go by without a single concert review.'

He concludes: 'Yet in the Far East a country like Taiwan (population 21 million) supports no less than *six* well-filled monthly magazines devoted to classical music and recordings. How many does America (population 270 million) have? Er, *none*. In the West, classical music has been sidelined by media bosses and decision makers who – desperately conscious of ratings – are guilty of a gross underestimation of public taste.'

Julian is convinced that, given half a chance, classical music has a vast potential audience, and cites the success of *Classic FM* in Britain and how, when BBC Television chose Puccini's *Nessun Dorma* as its 1990 World Cup theme, it topped the charts.

Julian's final words were electrifying: 'Today, I issue a challenge to the Breakfast TV companies – those arbiters of culture to the young. Give me four weeks of daily three-minute slots and I will deliver you twenty young musicians who will captivate your viewers. The results can then be recorded for CD and proceeds from the sales donated to a deserving musical charity or organisation. Western classical music is alive and kicking. But the television companies, the radio networks and the newspaper proprietors *have* to let the public know.'

The Times took up the argument and wrote a powerful leader outlining the major issues in Julian's speech. It begins with an example of taste in music enjoyed by the current resident of the White House when entertaining his counterpart from Downing Street. 'A decade ago the Prime Minister and the President of the United States might have dined in the White House to the strains of a string quartet. This week they sipped their *digestifs* to Elton John's 'Song for Guy' and Stevie Wonder's 'My Cherie Amour'. The choice may, however, say as much about wider perceptions of modern classical music as it does about what sits in the CD stacks of Downing Street and Pennsylvania Avenue.'

It goes on to outline Sir Simon Rattle's attempts to persuade the Government to support classical music and follows up many of Julian's points. The final paragraph says it all: 'There is no reason why classical music, if harmonious and melodious, cannot build new audiences for new work. If conductors and conservatories were to devote more time to nurturing new traditionalists they might find it easier to enlist the people on their side in the battle to persuade Mr Blair that *Be Here Now* is not the *ne plus ultra* of contemporary music.[99]

There was an immediate response from GMTV's Peter McHugh who phoned Julian in Davos to take him up on his challenge. He said: 'We can't give you a month, but we'll give you a week.' He explained that it was a move that could mean heavy financial penalties for GMTV if it failed because they are resposible to their advertisers if the ratings fall. Julian was adamant that the experiment would pay off, and said: 'I think the audience will be very surprised by how much they like the music and how taken they are with the performers.'[100]

Julian embarked on a hectic week, auditioning young musicians from all the colleges: 'I listened to hundreds of students and eventually selected ten musicians to come onto the programme. They were a good cross-section and included some well-known performers like the pianist Leif Ove Andsnes and the violinist Tasmin Little as well as students who had never played on television before. The whole thing was something young people could relate to.' The programme was a huge success with very high ratings, and GMTV confessed to getting the biggest post-bag they had ever received on any subject. 'Yet,' says Julian wryly, 'have they followed it up? Of course not. But I've proved it can work and I do think there has been a tiny bit of a shift in media coverage of classical music since then. But there is a very long way to go.' Three years after his speech Julian thinks that many of his prophecies have more than come true: 'When I made that speech a lot of people thought I went too far – but, in retrospect, I didn't go far enough. Many people in the business told me that they totally agreed with what I had said but would never dare to say so because of the repercussions. But if classical music is suffering, these topics need to be openly and urgently debated. Ironically, if my son wanted a career in music now I would give him the same advice that my father gave to Andrew and me for the situation is considerably worse today than when he advised us against entering the profession.'

Julian's speech created an enormous amount of interest, although he was misreported by many who said that he had attacked modern music. But analysis of the speech shows that Julian was attacking an attitude, which is something quite different. He criticised those who say you should only write one style of music: 'Because of that attitude we have missed out on a whole generation of British composers. Those who didn't want to go into another medium such as film music were just buried – like my father. There was a "mafia" who decreed that you had to write music like Stockhausen or you wouldn't get heard. And the general public had no say in how things progressed whatsoever.'

The writer Michael Kennedy made some significant remarks in his booklet notes for Julian's recording of Walton and Britten: 'The Walton Concerto was unlucky in its date. The late 1950s saw a fashionable rejection of romanticism and melody in favour of dry, unmelodious serialism. Composers like Walton were regarded by influential critics as an irrelevance, outdated and unimportant. Forty years later, it is serialism that has been rejected and Walton's music is again appreciated for its beauty and craftsmanship.'[101]

Andrew had reached his fiftieth birthday in April 1998 and Julian took part in a special celebratory concert at the Royal Albert Hall where he played two excerpts from *Variations*. It was a happy occasion with a packed and appreciative audience and Julian was particularly touched by the tribute Andrew paid to him in the programme. He wrote: 'I would like to thank my brother Julian for his loyalty and support when at times being my brother must have been – to put it mildly – a pain.' This was a welcome gesture as Andrew showed that he, too, appreciated the difficulties of Julian having to share a famous name.

Andrew's support came at a time when Julian was much in need of a helping hand as he was suffering from the effects of a continuing deeply disturbing personal crisis. The arguments between him and Zohra now dominated their lives and their relationship had become so tempestuous that the atmosphere was beginning to have an effect on David.

Julian says: 'There was an extraordinary magnetic force between Zohra and me that brought us together – then pushed us apart. We were both forceful characters. We wound each other up and brought out the worst in each other.' Zohra complained because she couldn't get Julian away from his work, and Julian complained because she did not seem interested enough to travel with him on tour. After one particularly violent argument, which was overheard by David, they knew that there was only one solution. Zohra and David moved out and stayed temporarily in Julian's mother's old flat next door. Julian remembers that their nineteen-year-old Spanish *au pair* Paula was very upset when the parting finally took place because her parents had split up when she was the same age as David. 'Both Paula and my assistant James Murphy were so helpful in moving all the things from one flat to the other. Their help went way beyond the call of duty throughout and I shall always be grateful to both of them for their kindness at this time.'

Julian was alone once more. This time, he was even more shattered for it meant that David, the son he adored, would no longer be with him. Zohra had agreed that, whatever happened, he would always have access, but the pain of the parting was extreme. Yet, Julian had to put his problems behind him for there were concerts and recording sessions looming ahead.

Despite the domestic situation, professionally there was much to raise Julian's spirits. When his CD comprising the complete cello and piano music of Delius and Grieg was released, it was universally greeted with enthusiasm. Once again, he had hit on the original idea of bringing together the music of two composers who had links both musically and personally. The Delius Sonata, Caprice, Elegy, Romance and *Serenade* from *Hassan* (arranged by Fenby) were placed alongside Grieg's *Intermezzo* and Sonata in A minor. Julian's partner on the piano for this recording was Bengt Forsberg with whom he had collaborated so successfully in 1996.

The *Daily Telegraph's* Geoffrey Norris writes of 'a great double act', outlining the fact that the two composers were friends for almost a quarter of a century and that it was Grieg who persuaded Delius's father to 'let young Fred continue his musical studies. For Delius, Grieg's music was like a breath of mountain air.'[102] The *Gramophone* cannot fault their performances and stress that they are 'splendidly matched' and furthermore: 'it is particularly good to have the tuneful Romance of 1898, written in Paris, which inexplicably remained neglected for 50 years until Lloyd Webber revived it.'[103] *BBC Music Magazine* was equally impressed, commenting on the 'well-matched partnership' where 'every dynamic, nuance and subtlety of tempo is delicately accomplished. The single-movement sonata is a particularly rewarding experience. Lloyd Webber caresses the music and plays it with passionate conviction.'[104]

Julian returned to Australia in August, this time to play the Elgar Concerto at the Brisbane Festival with the Academy of St Martin in the Fields conducted by Sir Neville Marriner. Clearly, the Australian audience had by now taken Julian to their hearts and the critics echoed their enthusiasm. Patricia Kelly in the *Brisbane Courier & Mail* comments: 'he glided into the Elgar, unfussy in his command of the performance yet sensitive to every nuance and gradation of tone.' She also makes an interesting comparison: 'The shadow of England's goddess of the cello, Jacqueline du Pré, will ever hang over the performances of the concerto she made her own, yet in this all-British performance Lloyd Webber did not try to outshine her demonstrative style but rather reinforced the memory in a quietly deferential way without losing the direct simplicity of his own confident voice in the very English harmonies and broodings of the concerto.'[105]

A further Festival performance of the Haydn C major Concerto with the Queensland Philharmonic Orchestra caused Kelly to pronounce that his playing was 'the cream of the night' and that 'technique vanished with the perfect weighting of Webber's bow over the strings and the quick-silver ease of fingers zipping up and down the fingerboard to meld Haydn's music in a mesmerising seamless flow.'[106]

By the autumn Julian was celebrating the release of another CD devoted to music written by his father. It not only re-confirmed what a talented composer he was, but was also indicative of Julian's persistence in making his music available. Entitled *Invocation*, it consists of ten works written over many years; *BBC Music Magazine* wrote of Lloyd Webber's 'gentle, subtle melodic gift, and his skill in compressing complex material, frequently employing unexpected developments, into short time spans.'[107] Not surprisingly, they consider *Aurora* to be the most impressive work on the disc.

In an interview by Andrew Achenbach for *Hi-Fi News & Record Review* prior to the release of the recording, Julian talks about his father's music and singles out the *Lento for Strings* as being the most extraordinary piece on the disc. 'It's the earliest composition here, but many people might think it the latest, so adventurous are the harmonies. The string writing is extraordinarily assured and it shows he was fully aware of what was happening on the European continent. For many years, I had no idea he'd written so much. In a sense we're almost listening to a new composer here; it's not that the music was neglected, it never even had the chance to be neglected! I personally can't understand the mentality of someone who could write a piece like the *Lento* and not be desperate to hear it played. I'll be surprised if the disc doesn't create a lot of interest.'[108] This was right but it is sad that Bill never lived to witness it.

Invocation was followed by a recording of some of Bill's chamber music and songs for Hyperion. This is a little gem of a disc with the Nash Ensemble bringing out every nuance with their usual high standard of performance. The songs are beautifully sung by John Mark Ainsley and show once again that Bill knew exactly how to write for the voice. There is no doubt that if he had been recognised earlier these songs could have stood proudly on a programme alongside those of Finzi or Vaughan Williams. Julian remembers the recording with both sadness and gratitude: gratitude to Ian Brown, who plays in every single item on the disc: 'Ian understood my father's music and the *Three Spring Miniatures* for Piano are beautifully played – as are the accompaniments to the songs', and sadness in that it was Christopher Van Kampen's last ever recording before he died so prematurely at the age of fifty-two. Christopher had been another pupil of Julian's teacher Douggie Cameron. Julian remembers: 'Chris was a consummate musician and part of the backbone of the musical scene for many years. He was a superb cellist, always reliable, always thoroughly prepared and always intensely interested in the music. At the time of the recording he was very ill but insisted that he would continue as long as he was given breaks to rest in between items. This disc is one I shall treasure for my father's music and Chris's beautiful playing.'

The producer of the recording was Andrew Keener and he gives some insight into the way Julian approached these sessions. 'In my experience, many composers who sit in on recordings of their music seldom contribute remarks on the "nuts and bolts" of a take – ensemble, intonation, dynamics etc. If a producer says: "how was that?" they tend to say "Fine, that was great" or make an overall comment about tempo. It seems sometimes that they are so happy to have their music recorded that they make few technical comments. Julian is not nearly so accommodating. He shares the producer's criteria and will question a passage here or a dynamic there. He will ask for a retake for the slightest thing that he feels is not right. I suppose in a way he is in the position of being a composer once removed. Since his father is no longer here to judge, he had to take on the responsibility and it worked.'

Gradually, people were taking more and more interest in William Lloyd Webber's music. Today it can be heard frequently on many radio stations but orchestras are not yet including it in the concert hall. Julian feels that *Aurora* should certainly be played but believes: 'My father will never be a "popular" composer because he didn't write enough music and he didn't write a big orchestral piece – there is no symphony. Miniaturists tend to be overlooked, and composers who write in this idiom are not taken seriously if they didn't write an epic work as well. On the other hand, his *Serenade for Strings* could easily be used as a theme for a film or TV series. It is just a question of time.' However, there is one work that Julian has discovered recently – in manuscript – which he thinks might redress the balance. It is an oratorio called *St. Francis of Assisi*. Written in 1948, it is one hour long and scored for strings, harp, choir and soloists.

Julian also thinks that there is prejudice against the Lloyd Webber name. Conductors are reluctant to play his music because they are scared that people will think they have only programmed it because of the name. 'It is bad enough for me, but it's worse for my father. At least I am a performer and can get out there and show them what I can do in a completely different way. But to be taken seriously as a composer when your son has had so much popular acclaim is difficult. Let's face it, if *Lento for Strings* had been written by Alban Berg it would have been played at the Proms years ago. And a lot of people working in the classical field – who have often not bothered to investigate it properly – dismiss Andrew's music, so they are prejudiced against his father before they have even begun to listen.'

Chapter 14

A Torch for Jackie

When Julian finds a cause, whether it be unearthing unjustly neglected music or making a stand against the way in which pop music has become the dominant musical culture, he will defend it against all odds. In January 1999 he sprang to the defence of that phenomenal young cellist Jacqueline du Pré, who at 28-years-old tragically had to abandon a brilliant career through multiple sclerosis and died at the age of 42.

Two years before, Jackie's sister Hilary and her brother Piers published a book called *A Genius in the Family* which one might have hoped would be a tribute to their sister's extraordinary talent. But this was not the case. The book gives a malicious account of her personal character in which she is depicted as selfish and foul-mouthed. She is also reputed to have had an affair with her brother-in-law, albeit with her sister's connivance. We see as the 'genius' not Jackie, but her sister Hilary, a flute player who *appeared* to show promise that was never fulfilled. Clearly, when Jackie's obvious talent eclipsed hers, Hilary became jealous and resented the attention bestowed upon her younger sister.

Alongside the book, Jackie's siblings were also working on the screenplay for a film called *Hilary and Jackie*. This so distorted the truth that it prompted a revolution among Jackie's musical colleagues. They had known and loved this girl who battled so bravely with disease and disappointment but still mustered what little energy she could to help other young musicians.

Julian thought that Jackie's sister and brother had perpetrated the ultimate act of betrayal and expressed his reaction in a *Daily Telegraph* article. He relates how, as an eleven-year-old, he was on a family holiday in a remote cottage near Lowestoft in Suffolk and heard du Pré for the first time: 'One morning my father announced that there was something on the radio that evening that I – as a budding cellist – should definitely listen to. It was to be a performance of the Elgar Cello Concerto from the Proms, played by a young girl called Jacqueline du Pré. This was an unusual request as my father rarely talked about music at all. Half past seven arrived and I found myself duly positioned by the radio set in the kitchen. I had heard little solo cello music before, so I had no idea of what to expect. I was certainly unprepared for the shattering effect of the opening chords and the extraordinary intensity of all that followed.'[109]

From this time onwards, Julian took every opportunity to hear du Pré play live and attended most of her London concerts. He well remembers her extraordinary platform presence and the magnetism that distinguished her from all other British musicians of her generation. When the book was published, Julian – who knew Jackie in her final years – was furious. When the film came out, he had reached boiling point. He wrote: '*Hilary and Jackie* is an ugly film, not because it is badly made or acted – quite the reverse – but because Emily Watson's du Pré bears no resemblance to the radiant Jackie I remember so well, first as a brilliant cellist, and later when I came to know her personally after she contracted MS. The film woefully fails to convey Jacqueline du Pré's wonderful joy in making music and her unique ability to bring that joy to her audience. Worst of all, the book that spawned the film was written by her elder sister, Hilary, and younger brother, Piers – two siblings apparently eaten up by bitterness and jealousy.'

The remainder of Julian's article deals aptly with all the 'bitterness and jealousy' and quotes some of the detail of this totally unsavoury portrayal of someone who cannot answer back. He then proceeded to contact many of his colleagues with the result that the following letter was published in *The Times* on 20 January, 1999:

> Sir, *Hilary and Jackie*, a film purporting to chronicle the life of cellist Jacqueline du Pré and based on a book by her brother and sister, is to be released this week. It concentrates heavily on an affair which Jacqueline had with her sister's husband and portrays her as selfish, spoilt and manipulative.
>
> This is not the Jacqueline du Pré that we, as her friends and colleagues, knew.
>
> Jacqueline possessed a wonderful joy in making music, and a unique ability to bring that joy to her audience. This is the Jacqueline du Pré that we remember.
>
> Yours,
>
> > Julian Lloyd Webber
> > Yehudi Menuhin
> > Itzhak Perlman
> > William Pleeth
> > M. Rostropovich
> > P. Zukerman[110]

The distasteful episode inspired Julian to compose a tribute to Jacqueline du Pré, which he called *Jackie's Song*. It was premièred at the Wigmore Hall a few days before the letter was published in *The Times*. *Jackie's Song* was also included, along with other short pieces, on a CD called *Cello Moods*. Jerrold Northrop Moore, (who was less than enthusiastic about

Jacqueline du Pré's later style) said that for him, the piece encapsulates the essential innocence of her early playing.

The matter might have ended there if it were not for the surprising intervention of Hilary's daughter, Clare Finzi, who had finally decided that she could no longer remain silent. She accused her parents of 'gross distortion' in order to make money and says that her father was a womaniser: 'Jackie comes over as the sole protagonist and Dad is portrayed as a gentle soul but my father had several affairs – tending to choose women who were lost and unsure of themselves. He was to them a wise, philosophical figure. As he had no boundaries it would end up with a sexual affair.'[111]

Julian was invited to appear on BBC Breakfast TV with the producer of the film, Andy Paterson. The previous evening, Julian had spoken to Clare Finzi: 'We talked the whole thing over and she said she would like to come on the programme with me so that she could "tell it how it really is." So I called the BBC and everything was arranged for her to be included. When they checked with Paterson he said that if she came on, he wouldn't. So he was wrong-footed from the start. I told him that his film had spent two hours maligning Jackie and that he had prevented Hilary's own daughter from talking for two minutes.'

The programme was revealing. What bothered Julian most was that all the posters declared *Hilary and Jackie* to be a true story. 'But now the director has back-tracked by saying that this is a mythical story. I think they would have been better to have put that on the posters instead of a "true story".' Paterson tried his best to defend the film but he was on very thin ground. 'It is a life-like story – a *section* of her life. I'm not trying to say it's the whole story.' Julian retaliated: 'It's based entirely on the memoirs of Hilary du Pré – but the book is extremely vicious. And you say you've consulted many people over the making of the film, but who have you consulted? Hilary du Pré and her brother, Piers.'

The presenter then brought up the main subject of the controversy, the affair between Jackie and her brother-in-law. Julian was quick off the mark: 'I feel very sorry about that because you must have known that Christopher Finzi had many affairs and that he had three children by two other women, but in the film it's Jackie who makes all the advances, which his own daughter says is a gross misrepresentation.' The presenter then suggested to Paterson that it is the salacious story that people are talking about and, of course, will remember. Paterson seemed unable to answer except to say that people outside the UK do not know what Jackie was like and when they see the film they will like what they see. Julian protested that that was just the trouble because if they didn't know anything about her private life they would take this as being accurate and that it was not true.

The film-makers employed various antics to try to make the film a success. They tricked their way into seeing William Pleeth, the teacher whom Jackie adored. Pleeth had signed the letter of protest to *The Times* so there was no way he condoned the *making* of the film (he already knew of the book and abhorred it). It seems that they had been in touch with the octogenarian Pleeth to say they were from Oxford and would like to talk to him about Jackie. Pleeth was under the impression that they were from Oxford University and were making some kind of documentary and agreed to see them. He was on his own when they arrived. The team included Emily Watson – who played Jackie in the film – and they proceeded to question him about Jackie's mannerisms, how she held the cello, etc. Pleeth naturally tried to be as helpful as possible.

But their *pièce de résistance* took place on the night of the film's première at the Barbican Centre. A Chinese girl called Wan Yeng Chen, who was still a student at the Royal College of Music received a phone call on the morning of the première asking if she would be prepared to go down to the Barbican that evening with her cello and play for a few minutes for a fee of £50. She was given no details, but a sum like that for a student is not to be refused.

Julian explained: 'When she arrived she was greeted by a girl from the Maclaurin Group – a PR firm employed by the film company – who showed her a banner on which was emblazoned the words "Leave Jackie Alone! Music Counts – Not Sex". She said to Wan Yeng: 'I'm going to hold this up and you'll play the cello underneath.' She duly performed and received her £50. When Emily Watson arrived she went straight over to Wan Yeng, while the photographers clicked merrily away. The following day many newspapers had a photo of the two of them, suggesting that Emily Watson had gone over to calm down the protestor. In reality, they had staged a fake protest to get publicity.

Julian comments: 'Unfortunately the truth about what really happened that night only came out six months later when I had spoken to Wan Yeng and she told me the whole story. I wish I had known her better because I could have warned her and they would have been in big trouble. As soon as she told me I gave her story to the *Evening Standard.'* Naturally, the newspaper could not resist such a gift and published an account under the heading 'Protester says Jackie demo was a fiddle.' They quote Wan Yeng: 'Somebody asked me to do the gig and I did it. I wasn't supposed to tell anybody about it. A girl paid me in cash. When I asked her to send me the next day's newspaper article, it arrived with a Maclaurin Group logo on the envelope.' When questioned by the *Evening Standard*, the group claimed ignorance, saying that the account director who had headed that team was no longer working for them.'[112]

David Mellor was among many who were impressed by Julian's forthright condemnation of the film. He admits that Julian's stand contributed to his own reluctance to see it for some time. When he finally saw it, he agreed with everything

Julian had said. Mellor, who has met and interviewed many famous musicians, admits that there are those who – although they might have strong opinions on particular subjects, which they will express privately – would refuse to put their views on record. 'Julian was not afraid. I think he led – most bravely – what was a highly successful counter attack. The annoying thing is that the film itself was quite well made and therefore the people who did not know Jackie would think that that was how she was and the wrong image remains.'

That June, Julian was invited along with the music commentator Norman Lebrecht to appear on *Channel 4 News* to discuss the appointment of Sir Simon Rattle as principal conductor of the Berlin Philharmonic Orchestra. This was a double triumph for British talent as the *Philharmonie* where the orchestra plays is not far from the new Reichstag building designed by the British architect Sir Norman Foster.

Lebrecht is one of the most articulate and outspoken of writers on music and on this occasion he and Julian were of a like mind. Both were obviously delighted that a young British conductor should have been chosen for this appointment, which had been previously held by legendary characters such as Wilhelm Furtwängler and Herbert von Karajan. Julian was overjoyed that British talent should be so recognised and said that nothing like this had happened since Barbirolli took over the conductorship of the New York Philharmonic from Arturo Toscanini half a century ago.

Lebrecht pointed out Simon Rattle's commitment to contemporary music, which meant that the German orchestra would be brought into the 21st century. Julian agreed that Rattle would inject new life into the repertoire of this great body of players. 'I think Simon will do a lot of new things – different kinds of music. He has done a great deal for music in this country. He's been very outspoken about music in schools and I think he will continue to do that. He will be a tremendous ambassador and this appointment has brought immense kudos to the country. It is a wonderful day for British music.'

Nonetheless Lebrecht stressed another side to this situation, reminding viewers that Simon Rattle was born in a 'semi' in Liverpool and that the Royal Liverpool Philharmonic Orchestra in his home town is at present starved of funding and on the brink of collapse. Once again, it is a sorry tale of the way the British – from government to the media – seem to ignore the importance of music in our lives.

In May 2000 Julian took part in a controversial event – the first Classical Brit Awards at the Royal Albert Hall. When Julian was presented with the Brit Award in 1987 for his recording of the Elgar Concerto he had reservations about the way the ceremony was presented. The classical award was squeezed in among the many pop categories and, as soon as it was announced, many of the pop industry moguls 'switched off' and started murmuring to each other at their dinner tables. Eventually, the British Phonographic Industry who present the Brits decided to dispense with the Classical award altogether. A decade later they created Classical Brits, which was televised by ITV and shown in their peak time evening slot. Julian says: 'Of course they wanted to sell it to TV and get high ratings, so they made it as popular as they could. The show began with Vanessa Mae, which I think gave a false impression. Although she is very good at what she does it isn't classical music. Nigel Kennedy was on the programme as well but the TV only showed him playing a salon piece while he wandered around the audience. But he had also played Massenet's *Meditation* from *Thaïs* beautifully. Charlotte Church and Lesley Garrett were also singing two songs but in each case the TV transmitted the "pop" one. I played *Jackie's Song* and a "samba" version of the A minor Paganini Caprice that I wrote with Pam Chowhan. We called it *Pagan Samba* and of course it was this, not *Jackie's Song,* which they showed on TV. There was a lot of controversy about the event but the complaints were based on the televised version. I think "Classical Brits" is a great idea but there is no need for TV companies to be frightened by beautiful pieces like Massenet's *Meditation.'*

Perhaps the BBC have got it right with 'Proms in the Park', another mass audience multi-media classical music event which Julian played at the following September. 'I played the first movement of the Elgar and Bach's *Air on a G String.* It was a fantastic experience to see 40,000 people enjoying every note of the evening. It is broadcast "live" on radio and TV every year and proves that classical music *can* have a huge popular appeal presented just as it is.'

Chapter 15

Quo Vadis?

Julian celebrated his fiftieth birthday on 14 April 2001. Three days later, at the Queen's Hall in Edinburgh, he premièred a new Cello Sonata, which he commissioned from James MacMillan. (MacMillan was one of the three contemporary composers singled out by Julian in his Davos speech.) Julian explains: 'He has a very strong individual voice and comes across as a composer who knows exactly what he's trying to say. And because he has such a strong vision it communicates to the listener. I've played his *Kiss on Wood* many times – a beautiful piece – so when I wanted a new recital item he was the obvious choice.'

Another composer much admired by Julian is the American Philip Glass and, in October 2001, Julian is due to première Glass's Cello Concerto in Beijing with the newly-formed China Philharmonic Orchestra – the first national orchestra in their history. Members are being drawn from all over the country and only the best players will be selected. Julian's involvement with the project began when he played at the Beijing Festival in 1999. His two concerts were sponsored by the Chinese telecommunications company, Xin de Telecom. Their managing director, the American William Krueger, asked Julian if he would like to return to the Festival two years later to première a new concerto by the composer of his choice. Julian had met Philip Glass in London a few months before and seized the opportunity to ask him to write a work for the occasion. In a magnificent philanthropic gesture, Krueger, together with his wife Rebecca, decided to commission Glass personally. The title page of the new concerto reads: 'Commissioned by William and Rebecca Krueger for Julian Lloyd Webber in honor of his 50th birthday with the world première performance by Maestro Yu Long and the China Philharmonic Orchestra on 21 October 2001 in Beijing.'

Prior to the Far Eastern event, on 1 June Julian will be taking part in a Fiftieth Birthday Celebration Concert in aid of the Prince's Trust at the Royal Albert Hall playing his beloved Elgar Cello Concerto. The programme will also include, significantly, music by William and Andrew Lloyd Webber.

If reaching fifty might herald a period of reflection for some, Julian would seem intent on looking to the future. 'People constantly ask me what I want to do now; what are my ambitions? My answer is – and always has been – that I want to go on doing exactly what I am doing. I love playing to people and bringing music to them. I enjoy travelling to places I've never been before, meeting interesting people and absorbing their cultures and I want to keep introducing new music for the cello. Yes, reaching fifty does provide an opportunity to reflect – but not for long! I certainly feel a lot of my family past has clarified itself now – particularly with the discovery of my father's music.'

The relationship between Julian and Andrew has always provided junk food for the media. Over the years they have probably had about as many disagreements as most siblings but in recent times, they seem to have rediscovered the closeness of their childhood. Andrew will be performing as guest artist at Julian's Fiftieth Birthday Concert (the first time they will have played together on stage). He also accompanies Julian in *Whistle Down the Wind* on the new CD

Julian Lloyd Webber plays Andrew Lloyd Webber. This is an updated version of the earlier disc, which has six new tracks from Andrew's latest musicals including *The Beautiful Game.* Julian reflects on their relationship: 'Andrew had to do it the hard way. When he left Oxford he did not get much support from either our mother or grandmother. My father was more understanding but, as with me, he made it clear to Andrew that there were not going to be any handouts. Andrew was only eighteen at the time and he worked tirelessly over the next three years with no tangible sign of success. When he suddenly earned a lot of money out of *Jesus Christ Superstar* I am not surprised that he didn't start throwing it around. But he gave me the most precious gift any composer can – his music – and I am proud to have played a part in the creation of *Variations.*'

During the researches for this book, the author discovered that Julian seems to be well-liked by his fellow musicians. Outside the profession his friends always comment on his unassuming personality. The former Arts Minister David Mellor says: 'Julian is one of those musicians – and there aren't too many of them – who get top marks as a human being as well as very much higher marks as a musician than some people, in the British way of denigrating success, would be willing to allow him. His friendship is important to me, not because he's a well-known musician (I've met many of those) but because I find him constantly interesting and absorbing. And the reason he is absorbing is because he is not play-acting. He is a real and genuine person. So many musicians are unable to relate to what is happening in the world about them. Musical talent can sometimes cut them off from the rest of the world and they can only come alive when they are doing what they know best, whereas Julian is genuinely in touch with everything that is happening in the world today. I still don't think he has been received as well as he deserves. He is concerned about many aspects of the musical scene. For instance, he is very concerned about the state of recording at the moment – not because he wants to record yet another Dvořák Concerto, but because he wants unjustly neglected works to be heard and recognised. Julian presents himself exactly as he is and has remained remarkably unspoiled.'

But have his many professional achievements been at the expense of his personal life? Although both his marriages have ended in divorce, Julian does not appear to rule out the possibility of a future partnership. When asked what he looks for in a woman, he is explicit: 'I don't want a personality that is on the surface and I don't like showy people. And – for some reason – I am not particularly attracted to women with money. I certainly look for a strong character and forceful personality. I don't like the "everything you do is wonderful" type. I like people who speak their minds and who are down to earth; people with ambitions in life, but not selfish ones. Above all, I need to be with a "believer" – I could not share my life with an atheist. But people are wrong when they say that someone so dedicated to their work cannot hope to have a successful marriage. It *is* possible. But you need a partner who is very understanding and supportive of what you are doing and they would need to have an interest of their own to pursue during all those terrible hours of practising! Experience has taught me a great deal. At last I have had some years of being alone. They have not been easy years but I have learned a tremendous amount from them and I now know that I *can* exist by myself. In the past I had always been part of a family. Within a year of leaving Harrington Court in 1973, Celia and I were married and, before I finally split up with Zohra, I had spent hardly a year of my life on my own. I was forty-six when that happened and it is a strange age to find yourself alone for the first time. If I marry again it *has* to be for the rest of my life. Whatever happens to me personally I have to be involved with music; it is my life-blood and I could not live with myself if I turned away from it for any selfish reason.'

Strong words from a single-minded character. *Quo Vadis?* may apply to Julian Lloyd Webber's personal life, but professionally he remains well and truly married to music.

Notes

All quotations are taken from author interviews, except for those referenced below.

1. *Andrew Lloyd Webber – His Life and Works* p 16.
2. *Cats On A Chandelier* p 22
3. *Travels With My Cello* p 3
4. *The Gower* Autumn 1967
5. *The Times* 13 May 1968
6. *Oh, What a Circus* pp 102–3
7. *Yorkshire Post* 18 Dec 1970
8. *Daily Telegraph* 8 Dec 1971
9. *Financial Times* 15 Dec 1971
10. *ibid.*
11. *Cats On A Chandelier* p 21
12. *Daily Telegraph* 30 Sept 1972
13. *Gramophone* March 1972
14. *The Times* 25 June 1976
15. *Gramophone* April 1977
16. Letter to MC
17. *Classical Music* 2 June 1979
18. *Birmingham Post* 30 April 1979
19. *Gramophone* Jan 1980
20. *Penguin Stereo & Cassette Record Guide 1980*
21. *Guardian* 3 Nov 1979
22. *New York Times* 17 Feb 1980
23. *Financial Times* 27 Aug 1980
24. *Daily Telegraph* 30 May 1981
25. *The Strad* July 1981
26. *Gramophone* May 1981
27. *Guardian* 11 Mar 1981
28. *The Herald* (Melbourne) 17 Oct 1985
29. *Evening Standard* 16 April 1982
30. *Observer* 16 April 1982
31. *Sunday Telegraph* 18 April 1982
32. *Gramophone* Aug 1982
33. *Fanfare* Jan 1983
34. *Sunday Times* 19 June 1983
35. *Guardian* 24 June 1983
36. *Gramophone* June 1983
37. *New York Times* 1 Jan 1984
38. *Detroit Free Press* 7 Jan 1984
39. *Die Welt* (trans) 9 Feb 1984
40. *Daily Telegraph* 15 Sept 1986
41. *Music & Musicians* Oct 1986
42. *Sunday Times* (Perth) 13 Oct 1985
43. *Sydney Morning Herald* 14 Oct 1985
44. *Japan Times* 2 Nov 1986
45. *Guardian* 13 Feb 87
46. *Daily Telegraph* 17 Aug 1987
47. *Courier Mail* 19 Aug 1987
48. *Guardian* 15 Dec 1987
49. *Financial Times* 15 Dec 1987

50. *Music & Musicians* Jan 1988
51. *Gramophone* Jan 1988
52. *Irish Times* 10 May 1985
53. *Classical Music* 11 June 1988
54. *Washington Post* 12 Oct 1989
55. *Australian* 12 Sept 1990
56. *Sydney Morning Herald* 13 Sept 1990
57. *Washington Post* 1 Aug 1991
58. *BBC Music Magazine* August 1992
59. Letter to MC
60. *The Cello and the Nightingale*
61. *Salzburg Volkszeitung* 18 Feb 1993
62. *Classical Music* 27 Mar 1993
63. *Gramophone* October 1993
64. *The Sunday Times* 29 Oct 2000
65. *Washington Post* 18 Jan 1994
66. *Time Out* 14–21 Dec 1994
67. *The Lady* 13–19 Dec 1994
68. *Sunday Telegraph* 5 Feb 1995
69. *Classic FM* March 1995
70. *Stereo Review* Aug 1995
71. Letter to MC
72. Letter to MC
73. *Miami Herald* 14 June 1994
74. Letter to MC
75. *Daily Telegraph* 15 Feb 1995
76. *Daily Telegraph* 2 Nov 1995
77. *Independent* 29 Nov 1995
78. *Guardian* 27 Nov 1995
79. *Gramophone* Nov 1996
80. *Evening Standard* 7 Nov 1996
81. *The Strad* (Roderic Dunnett) April 1997
82. *Evening Standard* 13 Oct 1997
83. *Guardian* 10 Mar 1997
84. *The Times* 10 Mar 1997
85. *Observer* 16 Mar 1997
86. *The Strad* July 1997
87. *Observer* 9 Nov 1997
88. Letter to MC
89. *Gramophone* Aug 1997
90. *Classic CD* Aug 1997
91. *Independent on Sunday* 22 June 1997
92. *Sunday Telegraph* 29 June 1997
93. *Daily Mail* 8 Aug 1997
94. *Daily Telegraph* 20 Sept 1997
95. *The Strad* Dec 1997
96. *Gramophone* Nov 1997
97. *Classic CD* Nov 1997
98. *The Strad* Dec 1997
99. *The Times* 7 Feb 1998
100. *Daily Telegraph* 16 Feb 1998
101. Booklet with CD (Philips)
102. *Daily Telegraph* 31 Jan 1998
103. *Gramophone* April 1998
104. *BBC Music Magazine* April 1998
105. *Brisbane Courier & Mail* 31 Aug 1998
106. *Brisbane Courier & Mail* 5 Sept 1998
107. *BBC Music Magazine* Sept 1998
108. *Hi-Fi News & Record Review* May 1998
109. *Daily Telegraph* 4 Jan 1999
110. *The Times* 20 Jan 1999
111. *The Times* 21 Jan 1999
112. *Evening Standard* 18 June 1999

JULIAN LLOYD WEBBER

DISCOGRAPHY
Recordings with Orchestra

Favourite Cello Concertos – two CD set
Elgar – Cello Concerto; Dvořák – Cello Concerto; Saint-Saëns
– Cello Concerto; Tchaikovksy – *Rococo Variations* other works
for cello and orchestra
Philips CD 462 505-2

Dvořák Cello Concerto
Czech Philharmonic Orchestra / Vaclav Neumann
Philips CD / MC / LP 422 387-2 / 4 / 1

Elgar Cello Concerto
Royal Philharmonic Orchestra / Sir Yehudi Menuhin
Philips CD / MC / LP 416 354-2

Britten Cello Symphony
Walton Cello Concerto
Academy of St. Martin-in-the-Fields / Sir Neville Marriner
Philips CD 454 442-2

Saint-Saëns Cello Concerto
Honegger Cello Concerto
Fauré *Élégie*
D'Indy *Lied* (world première recording)
Saint-Saëns *Allegro Appassionato*
English Chamber Orchestra / Yan Pascal Tortelier
Philips CD / MC 432 084-2 / 4

Celebration – two CD set
Rodrigo *Concierto como un Divertimento* (world première recording)
Lalo Cello Concerto
London Philharmonic Orchestra / Jesus Lopez-Cobos

Delius Cello Concerto
Holst *Invocation* (world première recording)
Vaughan Williams *Fantasia on Sussex Folk Tunes* (world première recording)
Philharmonia Orchestra / Vernon Handley

Canteloube – *Bailero* (Shepherd's Song); De Falla – *Ritual Fire Dance*; Saint-Saëns – *Softly Awakes My Heart* (from *Samson and Delilah*); Bridge – *Scherzetto*; Fauré – *Élegie*; Villa-Lobos – *Bachianas Brasilieras No. 5*; J.S. Bach – *Arioso*; Popper – Gavotte No. 2; Delius – *Serenade* from *Hassan*; Bruch – *Kol Nidrei*
National Philharmonic Orchestra / Charles Gerhardt
BMG 74321 84112 2

Tchaikovsky *Variations on a Rococo Theme* (composer's version)
Miaskovsky Cello Concerto
Shostakovich *The Limpid Stream*
Tchaikovsky Nocturne in D minor
London Symphony Orchestra / Maxim Shostakovich
Philips CD 434 106-2

Elgar Cello Concerto
Walton Cello Concerto
Royal Philharmonic Orchestra – Sir Yehudi Menuhin
Academy of St. Martin in the Fields – Sir Neville Marriner
Philips 464 700-2

Gavin Bryars Cello Concerto (*Farewell to Philosophy*)
(world première recording)
English Chamber Orchestra/James Judd
Philips CD/MC 454 126-2/4

Nyman Concerto for Cello and Saxophone
(world première recording)
John Harle (saxophone)/Philharmonia Orchestra/Michael
Nyman
EMI CDC 5 564872

Bantock *Sapphic Poem* for Cello and Orchestra
(world première recording)
Royal Philharmonic Orchestra/Vernon Handley
Hyperion CDA66899

Delius Caprice and Elegy
Royal Philharmonic Orchestra/Eric Fenby
Unicorn-Kanchana CD/MC/LP CD RT/RT/DKP 9008/9B

Bridge Oration (*Concerto Elegiaco*) for Cello and Orchestra
(world première recording)
London Philharmonic Orchestra/Nicholas Braithwaite
Lyrita LP SRCS 104

Sullivan Cello Concerto (world première recording)
Herbert Cello Concerto No. 2
Elgar Romance
London Symphony Orchestra/Sir Charles Mackerras
EMI CD/MC/LP CDC 747 622-2 EL 270 430-4/1

Sullivan Cello Concerto (world première recording)
Julian Lloyd Webber, London Symphony Orchestra, Sir
Charles Mackerras
EMI CLASSICS 7 64726 2

Travels with My Cello
Rimsky-Korsakov – *The Flight of the Bumblebee*; Lehar – *Vilja-Lied* (from *The Merry Widow*); Debussy – *Golliwog's Cake-walk*;
Schumann – *Traumerei*; Albeniz – *Puerta de tierra*; Saint-Saëns
– *Le Cygne*; Bach/Gounod – *Ave Maria*; William Lloyd Webber
– *Andante Affettuoso*; Johann/Josef Strauss – *Pizzicato Polka*;
Albinoni/Giazotto – Adagio; Grainger – *Irish Tune from
County Derry*; Khatchaturian – *Sabre Dance*
English Chamber Orchestra/Nicholas Cleobury
Philips CD/MC 412 231-2/4

Encore! (*Travels with My Cello* – Volume 2)
Gershwin – 'Bess, You is My Woman Now' (from *Porgy and
Bess*); Taube – Nocturne; Mozart – *Rondo alla Turca*; Debussy –
Clair de Lune; Trad. – *Skye Boat Song*; Bizet – *Habanera* (from
Carmen); Vangelis – *Un Après-midi*; Narita – *Song of the
Seashore*; Lennon/McCartney – 'When I'm Sixty-four';
Bernstein – 'Somewhere' (from *West Side Story*); Bach – *Jesu,
Joy of Man's Desiring*; Rimsky-Korsakov – *Chant Hindou* (from
Sadko); Lehar – *You are My Heart's Delight*
Royal Philharmonic Orchestra/Nicholas Cleobury
Philips CD 416 698-2

Andrew Lloyd Webber *Variations*
London Philharmonic Orchestra/Lorin Maazel
Philips CD/MC/LP 420 342-2/4/1

Julian Lloyd Webber plays Andrew Lloyd Webber
Variations 1-4; 'The Phantom of the Opera'; 'Love Changes

Everything'; 'Memory'; 'I Don't Know How to Love Him'; 'Starlight Express'; 'Music of the Night'; 'Buenos Aires'; 'Don't Cry For Me Argentina'; 'All I Ask of You'; 'Tell Me on a Sunday'; 'Close Every Door'; 'John 19:41'; 'Pie Jesu'; 'With One Look'; 'God's Own Country'; 'The Perfect Year'; 'Our Kind of Love'; 'Whistle Down The Wind'; 'No Matter What'
Royal Philharmonic Orchestra/Barry Wordsworth
Philips Classics 468362-2

English Idyll
Delius – Caprice and Elegy; Dyson – Fantasy for Cello and Orchestra (world première recording); Elgar – Idyll for Cello and Organ; Elgar – Romance Op. 62; Grainger – *Youthful Rapture*; Grainger – *Brigg Fair*; Holst – *Invocation*; Ireland – *The Holy Boy*; Cyril Scott – *Pastoral and Reel*; Vaughan Williams – *Romanza* from *Tuba Concerto* (arr. the composer); Walford Davies – *Solemn Melody*
Academy of St. Martin-in-the-Fields/Sir Neville Marriner
Philips CD 442 530-2

The Julian Lloyd Webber Collection
Lloyd Webber – *South Bank Show* theme; Saint-Saëns – *The Swan*; Mozart – *Rondo alla Turca*; Debussy – *Clair de Lune*; Bach/Gounod – *Ave Maria*; Vangelis – *Un Après-midi*; Lloyd Webber – 'Love Changes Everything'; Lennon/McCartney – 'When I'm Sixty-Four'; Trad. – *Skye Boat Song*; Albinoni – Adagio; Lloyd Webber – 'Music of the Night'; Bernstein – 'Somewhere'; Bach – *Jesu, Joy of Man's Desiring*; Rimsky-Korsakov – *Chant Hindou*; Lehar – *You are My Heart's Delight*; Rimsky-Korsakov – *The Flight of the Bumblebee*; Johann/Josef Strauss – *Pizzicato Polka*; Schumann – *Träumerei*; Trad. (arr. Grainger) – *Londonderry Air* (Danny Boy); Elgar – Cello Concerto, first movement
Philips CD 446 050-2

Elegy
Fauré – *Élégie*; Albinoni – Adagio; Saint-Saëns – *Le Cygne*;
Taube – Nocturne; Bach – *Jesu, Joy of Man's Desiring*; Rimsky-
Korsakov – *Chant Hindou*; Debussy – *Clair de Lune*;
Bach/Gounod – *Ave Maria*; Elgar – Cello Concerto, first
movement; Debussy – *Beau Soir*; Dvořák – *Songs my Mother
Taught Me*; Grieg – *To Spring*; Bach – Adagio; Schumann –
Träumerei; Canteloube – *Brezairola*; Villa-Lobos – *Song of the
Black Swan*; Hewitt – *Shepherd's Lullaby*; San-Lang – *Itsuki
Lullaby*; Lloyd Webber – 'Pie Jesu'
Philips CD 462 712-2

Cello Moods
Franck – *Panis Angelicus*; Elgar – *Chanson du Matin*; Elgar –
Salut d'amour; Julian Lloyd Webber – *Jackie's Song*; Debussy –
Reverie; Bach – *Air on a G String*; Massenet – *Meditation* (from
Thaïs; Japanese trad. – *Sakura, Sakura*; Caccini – Ave Maria;
Borodin – Nocturne; Glazunov – *Melodie*; Chopin – Nocturne
in E Op. 9 No. 2; Boccherini – Adagio from Concerto in B♭;
Rheinberger – *Cantilena* (from) Organ Sonata in D minor;
Bruch – *Kol Nidrei*
Royal Philharmonic Orchestra/James Judd
Philips CD/MC 462 588-2/4

Dirk Brossé
Elegy for Cello and Orchestra, London Philharmonic
Orchestra/Brossé
Philips 465274-2

Two Worlds
Bach – *Siciliana*
Villa-Lobos – *Bachianas Brasileiras* No. 4 – Preludio
with Lee Ritenour (guitar) & Dave Grusin (piano)
Decca CD 467 132-2

Recital Recordings

Britten Sonata in C Op. 65
Shostakovich Sonata for Cello and Piano
Prokofiev *Ballade*
John McCabe (piano)
Philips CD 422 345-2

Grieg Sonata for Cello and Piano; *Intermezzo*
Delius Sonata for Cello and Piano; Caprice & Elegy; *Serenade*
from *Hassan*; Romance
Bengt Forsberg (piano)
Philips CD 454 458-2

Rachmaninov Sonata for Cello and Piano
Debussy Sonata for Cello and Piano
Rachmaninov Prelude for Cello and Piano (world première
recording); *Danse Orientale*
Yitkin Seow (piano)
ASV MC/LP ZC/– ALH 911

Fricker Sonata for Cello and Piano
Berkeley Duo for Cello and Piano
McCabe Partita for Solo Cello
Dalby Variations for Cello and Piano
(all world première recordings)
John McCabe (piano)
L'Oiseau-Lyre LP DSLO 18

Delius Cello Sonata
Eric Fenby (piano) Unicorn-Kanchana UKCD 2074

The Romantic Cello
Popper – *Elfentanz*; Saint-Saëns – *Le Cygne*; Mendelssohn –
Song Without Words; Delius – Romance; Saint-Saëns – *Allegro*

Appassionato; Rachmaninov – Andante (from Sonata for Cello and Piano); Elgar – *Salut d'amour*; Fauré – *Après un Rêve*; Chopin – *Introduction and Polonaise Brillante*
Yitkin Seow (piano)
ASV CD/MC/LP CD/ZC/- ACM 2002

Stanford Cello Sonata No. 2 (world première recording)
Ireland Sonata for Cello and Piano
Bridge *Elegy; Scherzetto* (world première recordings)
John McCabe (piano)
ASV CD CD DCA 807

Rawsthorne Sonata for Cello and Piano
Britten Third Suite for Cello (world première recording)
Arnold *Fantasy for Cello* (world première recording)
Britten *Tema Sacher* (world première recording)
Ireland *The Holy Boy*
John McCabe (piano)
ASV CD DCA592

Music of William Lloyd Webber
William Lloyd Webber: *Three pieces* for Cello and Piano
John Lill (piano)
ASV CD DCA 961

Invocation
William Lloyd Webber: *Nocturne* for Cello and Harp
Skaila Kanga (harp)
Chandos CD CHAN 9595

Andrew Lloyd Webber – *Variations* (world première recording)
CD MCLD 19396

Début
J.S. Bach – *Bourrees* (from Suite No. 3); Boccherini – *Rondo*

(from String Quintet op. 32 No. 7 arr. Schroeder); Beethoven – first movement from Cello Sonata No. 4; Popper – Gavotte No. 2; Saint-Saëns – *Allegro Appassionata*; Fauré – *Elegie*; Delius – Cello Sonata
Clifford Benson (piano)
CBS LP MP 42235

Ireland Phantasie Trio in A minor
          Trios nos. 2 and 3
Yfrah Neaman (violin); Eric Parkin (piano)

Cello Song
Villa-Lobos – *Song of the Black Swan*; J.S. Bach – Adagio (from Cantata BWV 156); Castelnuovo-Tedesco – *Sea Murmurs* (arr. Heifetz); Schumann – *Langsam* (from Five Pieces in folk style); Scriabin – Etude op. 8 no. 11 (arr. Piatigorsky); Rachmaninov – Romance (1890); Grieg –*To Spring*; Delius – *Serenade* from *Hassan* (arr. Fenby); Elgar – Romance Op. 62; Chopin – *Largo* (from Sonata for Cello and Piano Op. 65); Brahms – *Wie Melodien zieht es mir*; Dvořák – *Songs My Mother Taught Me* Op. 55 No. 4; Trad. – *Star of County Down* (arr. J. Lloyd Webber); Debussy – *Beau Soir* (arr. Heifetz); Messiaen – *Louange à l'éternité de Jésus* (from *Quatuor Pour La Fin du Temps*)
John Lenehan (piano)
Philips CD/DCC/MC 434 017-2/5/4

Cradle Song
Julian Lloyd Webber – *Song for Baba*; Schumann – *Träumerei*; Schubert – *Wiegenlied*; Montsalvatge – *Cradle Song*; Hewitt – *Shepherd's Lullaby*; Dvořák – *Wiegenlied*; Dvořák – *Songs My Mother Taught Me*; Richard Rodney Bennett – *Dream Sequence*; Quilter – *Slumber Song*; Cyril Scott – *Lullaby*; William Lloyd Webber – *Slumber Song*; Quilter – *Where Go The Boats*; Canteloube – *Brezairola*; Khachaturian – *A Little Song*; John Lenehan – *Alice*; Poulenc – (excerpt from) *Babar the Elephant*;

Dave Heath – *Gentle Dreams*; **John Rutter** – *Mary's Lullaby*; Fauré – *Dolly Suite*; Brahms – *Wiegenlied*; Nursery Suite (arr. by Pam Chowhan)
John Lenehan (piano); Richard Rodney Bennett (piano); Pam Chowhan (piano)
Philips CD/MC 442 426-2/4

William Lloyd Webber's Principal Compositions

William Lloyd Webber's earliest compositions date from 1936 when he wrote his *Fantasy Trio*. From 1945 to the mid-fifties he wrote music in a variety of forms, vocal, instrumental, choral, organ, chamber and orchestral. Works from this period include the oratorio, *St. Francis of Assisi*, the orchestral tone poem, *Aurora*, the sonatinas for viola and piano and flute and piano, numerous songs, organ pieces and choral works.

Disillusioned with composition (see Chapter 4), he wrote virtually nothing for the next twenty years until, shortly before his death, a sudden flowering of creativity produced a number of works including the *Missa Santae Mariae Magdalenae* (see Chapter 7).

The possessor of a remarkable melodic gift, which he frequently allied with surprisingly 'purple' harmonies, he was a composer who knew exactly what he wanted to say and how to say it. When *Aurora* was recorded for Philips in 1986 by Lorin Maazel and the London Philharmonic Orchestra, it was a revelation. Edward Greenfield of the *Guardian* called it 'skilfully and sumptuously scored...music as sensuous as any you will find from a British composer.' Yet his music remained virtually undiscovered until recently when works which had lain unpublished and unperformed for many years have gradually come to light.

William Southcombe Lloyd Webber (b. London 11 March 1914, d. London 29 October 1982). Educated at Mercer's School where he was scholar organist. Won open scholarship to the Royal College of Music (1931), F.R.C.O (1933), D. Mus. (1939). Appointments: Organist, Christ Church, Newgate Street (1931–2). Organist St. Cyprian's, Clarence Gate, (1933–9). Organist and choirmaster of the Resident Choir School, All Saints, Margaret' Street, (1929–48). Professor and examiner, Royal College of Music, (1946–82). Examiner for the Associated Board of the Royal Schools of Music (1946–82). Organist and Director of Music, Central Hall, Westminster (1958–82). Director of London College of Music (1964–82). Master of the Worshipful Company of Musicians (1973–4). Civic Guild of Old Mercers (1978). Honours: CBE 1980.

William Lloyd Webber Discography

Music by William Lloyd Webber.
Artists include John Lill, Philip Dukes, Richard Hickox, Julian Lloyd Webber
ASV CD DCA 961 (1996)

Organ Works of William Lloyd Webber
Jane Watts plays the Willis Organ of Salisbury Cathedral
Priory PRCD 616 (1997)

William Lloyd Webber Chamber Music & Songs
John Mark Ainsley & The Nash Ensemble
Hyperion CDA 67008 (1997)

William Lloyd Webber Invocation
City of London Sinfonia, Richard Hickox, Tasmin Little,
Skaila Kanga, Ian Watson, Julian Lloyd Webber, The
Westminster Singers, Choir of the Arts Educational School,
London. Gareth Jones, Hollie Cook.
Chandos CHAN 9595 (1998)

Sacred Choral Music of William Lloyd Webber
The Choir of All Saints, Margaret Street, London. Directed by
Harry Bramma.
Priory PRCD 677 (1999)

William Lloyd Webber – A List of Works

Work	Publisher
ORCHESTRAL	
Aurora	(Chester Music)
Three Spring Miniatures	(Chester Music)
Lento for Strings	(Chester Music)
Serenade for Strings	(Chester Music)
Invocation	(Chester Music)

INSTRUMENTAL

Cello and piano
Nocturne (Stainer & Bell)
Three Pieces (Stainer & Bell)
In the Half-Light; Air Varié; Slumber Song

Clarinet and piano
Air and Variations (Stainer & Bell)
Frensham Pond (Stainer & Bell)

Flute and piano
Sonatina (Peters)
Mulberry Cottage (Peters)

Horn and piano
Summer Pastures (Stainer & Bell)

Piano Trio
Fantasy Trio (Stainer & Bell)

Trumpet and piano
Suite in B flat (Stainer & Bell)

Viola and piano
Sonatina (Stainer & Bell)

Violin and harp/piano
The Gardens at Eastwell (Stainer & Bell)

Violin and organ
Benedictus (Stainer & Bell)

PIANO

Three Spring Miniatures (William Elkin)
Six Pieces (Kevin Mayhew)
A Song for the Morning; Scherzo in G minor; Arabesque; Romantic Evening; Explanation; Song without Words
Three Pieces (Kevin Mayhew)
Presto for Perseus; Autumn Elf; Badinage de Noël
Scenes from Childhood (Kevin Mayhew)
Cake Walk; Sentimental Waltz; Air; Scherzo; Evening Hymn; China Doll; A Short Tone-Study

CHORAL

Missa Sanctae Mariae Magdalenae (Kevin Mayhew)
– Mass
Princeps Pacis (The Prince of Peace) (Kevin Mayhew)
– Mass
The Saviour (Music Sales)
– A meditation upon the death of Christ

The Divine Compassion	(Kevin Mayhew)
– A sacred cantata	
St. Francis of Assisi	(In preparation)
– An oratorio	

ANTHEMS

O Lord, Spread thy Wings o'er me	(Chester Music)
Spirit of God	(Kevin Mayhew)
Dominus Firmamentum Meum	(Kevin Mayhew)
Lo! My Shepherd is Divine	(Kevin Mayhew)
Lo! God is Here	(Music Sales)
Love divine, all Loves Excelling	(Music Sales)

VOCAL

The Songs of William Lloyd Webber   (Kevin Mayhew)
'I looked out into the Morning'; 'Over the Bridge'; 'How do I love Thee'; 'The Forest of Wild Thyme'; 'The pretty Washer-Maiden'; 'A Rent for Love'; 'To the Wicklow Hills'; 'So Lovely the Rose'; 'Eutopia'; 'The Cottage of Dreams'

CAROLS

'Jesus, Dear Jesus'   (Chester Music)
'The Stable where the Oxen stood (The Manger Bright)'
                                                 (Kevin Mayhew)
'Then come, all Ye People'   (Kevin Mayhew)

ORGAN

Chorale, Cantilena & Finale	(Kevin Mayhew)
Three Recital Pieces	(Kevin Mayhew)

Prelude; Barcarolle; Nuptial March
Aria – Thirteen Pieces for organ   (Kevin Mayhew)
Prelude on St Cross; Choral March; Communion; Solemn Procession; Prelude on Passion Chorale; Prelude on Rockingham; Festal March; Prelude on Gerontius; Aria; Verset for Organ; Prelude on Winchester New; Vesper Hymn; Meditation on Stracathro

Reflections – Seven Pieces for Organ   (Kevin Mayhew) Prelude;
Slumber Song; Summer Pastures; Romance; Intermezzo; *Christ
in the Tomb* (from *The Divine Compassion*); Postlude
Eight Varied Pieces for Organ   (Bosworth)
Arietta in A major; Minuet; Recessional; *Andantino alla
Cantilena; Introit; Dedication March;* Pastorale; Epilogue
Songs without Words – Six Pieces for Organ   (Chester Music)
'Noël Nouvelet'; 'Song without Words'; Trumpet Minuet;
'God Rest You Merry Gentlemen'; 'The Coventry Carol';
'Good King Wenceslas'
Five Portraits for Home Organs   (Music Sales)

PUBLISHERS

Please contact your local music retailer for publications, or in
the event of difficulty please contact:

Chester Music Ltd.
8/9 Frith Street
London W1D 3JB
Tel: 020 7434 0066
Fax: 020 7287 6329
Website: www.musicsales.co.uk
e-mail: music@musicsales.co.uk

Music Sales Ltd.
8/9 Frith Street
London W1D 3JB
Tel: 020 7434 0066
Fax: 020 7287 6329
Website: www.musicsales.co.uk
e-mail: music@musicsales.co.uk

Stainer & Bell Ltd.
PO Box 110
Victoria House
23 Gruneisen Road
Finchley
London N3 1DZ
Tel: 020 8343 3303
Fax: 020 8343 3024
Website: www.stainer.co.uk
e-mail: post@stainer.co.uk

Kevin Mayhew Ltd.
Buxhall
Stowmarket
Suffolk IP14 3BW
Tel: 01449 737978
Fax: 01449 737834
Website: www.kevinmayhewltd.com
e-mail: info@kevinmayhewltd.com
          sales@kevinmayhewltd.com

Peters Edition Ltd.
10-12 Baches Street
London N1 6DN
Tel: 020 7553 4000
Fax: 020 7490 4921
Website: www.edition-peters.com
e-mail: sales@uk.edition-peters.com

Bibliography

Campbell, Margaret, *The Great Cellists*. London, Victor Gollancz, 1988.

Coveny, Michael, *Cats on a Chandelier*. London, Hutchinson, 1999.

du Pré, Hilary & Piers, *A Genius in the Family*. London, Chatto & Windus, 1997.

Harrison, Beatrice (ed. Patricia Cleveland-Peck), *The Cello and the Nightingales*. London, John Murray, 1985.

Lloyd Webber, Julian, *Short Sharp Shocks*. London, Weidenfeld & Nicolson, 1990.

Lloyd Webber, Julian, *Song of the Birds*. London, Robson Books, 1985.

Lloyd Webber, Julian, *Travels with my Cello*. London, Pavilion Books, 1984.

Rice, Tim, *Oh, What A Circus*. London, Coronet, 1999.

Walsh, Michael, *Andrew Lloyd Webber – His Life & Works*. London, Viking Penguin 1989.

Index